REFERENCE USE ONLY

Sunset Travel Guide to
Arizona

By the Editors of *Sunset Books* and *Sunset Magazine*

Lane Publishing Co., Menlo Park, California

Hours, admission fees, prices, telephone numbers, and highway designations in the editorial content of this book are accurate as of September 1978.

Acknowledgments:

We are grateful to the many people and organizations who assisted in the preparation of this travel guide. Officials of various local, state, and federal agencies and state and national recreation areas and monuments, as well as many other individuals throughout the state, gave invaluable help in compiling and verifying factual information in this book.

Supervising Editors: René Klein and Dorothy Krell
Text and Research: Thomas D. Boyd

Design: John Flack
Cartography: Ted Martine and Jack Doonan
Cover: Ancient cliff dwellings of Betatakin in Navajo National Monument. Photograph by Glenn Christiansen.

Editor, Sunset Books: David E. Clark

Contents

Special features

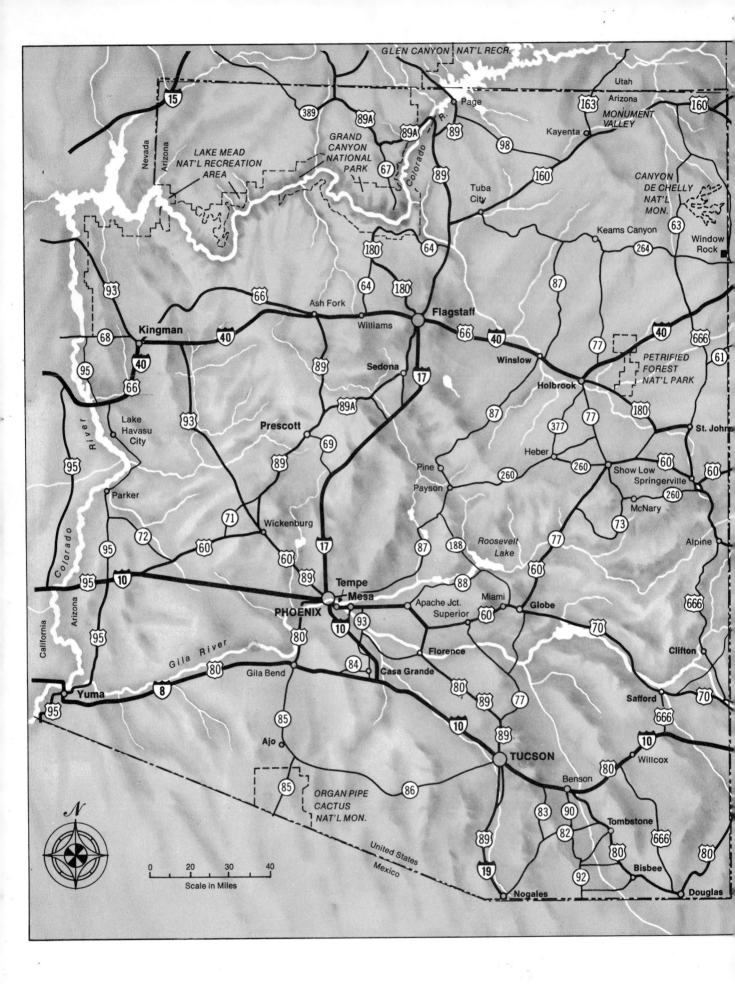

An introduction to Arizona

Since World War II, Arizona has been one of the nation's fastest growing states. Phoenix and Tucson have doubled and redoubled their population in the last 30 years, new industry has continued to develop, and retired people are moving to Arizona from all parts of the country. Yet despite all this growth, Arizona is still the "wide open spaces" and will remain so for a long time to come.

Arizona's wide-open spaces come in a variety that surprises many visitors. The state is not all desert. At Flagstaff, more than a mile high, snowstorms sometimes blanket the city in early May, and in the White Mountain lakes a popular winter sport is ice-fishing. The number of lakes, too, is a surprise; one result is that Arizona has more boats per capita than any other state in the union.

Winter or summer, Arizona has something to tempt the tourist. For the vacationer who wants to eat well, sleep late, and sit in the sun, Arizona's resorts provide all the comforts. Long a favorite destination for winter sun-seekers, Arizona offers a wide range of resort accommodations from the very simple to the most luxurious.

The more active visitor finds ample opportunity for fishing, picnics in the desert, hiking, skiing, riding, and auto exploring. Amateur geologists can spend many field days poking around the countryside. Plant lovers will discover the saguaro, cholla, prickly pear, yucca, and forests of pine and juniper. History-minded travelers have innumerable historical monuments and archeological ruins to explore, many of which tell the story of an Indian population that thrived hundreds of years before Columbus was born.

Climate

Arizona can be classified in five climate zones based on elevation. The low-lying Sonora desert occupies southwestern Arizona and follows the Colorado River, with an enclave in the southeast corner (Yuma, Parker, Lake Havasu City, Phoenix and vicinity, Gila Bend, Ajo, Page, Safford). Normal summer temperatures range from 72° to over 100°, topping 110° in some places. Winter ranges from 39° to 67°, rarely below freezing. The high desert foothills (Tucson, Nogales, Benson, Tombstone, Douglas, Winslow, Wickenburg, Prescott) are cooler, normally from 63° to 94° in summer and 31° to 59° in winter. The warm highlands (Prescott, Payson, the Tonto Basin, the Apache reservations, and scattered areas of the southeast) range from 27° to 57° in the winter and 61° to 92° in the summer. The cool highlands, mountains above 6,500 feet (Williams, Flagstaff, the Mogollon Rim, the White Mountains and the Chuska Mountains east of Canyon de Chelly) are refreshing in summer, normally from 44° to 78°, and often under deep snow in winter, with normal temperatures from 14° to 44°. The high plateau of the northwest (the Navajo and Hopi reservations and the strip north of the Mogollon Rim) normally range from 60° to 94° in summer and 27° to 55° in winter, with light snow that often melts between snowfalls.

Late fall, winter, and spring bring most visitors to the desert, and summer makes the mountains popular. Throughout the state, summer thunderstorms and brief, heavy rains occur in July and August; they are heaviest in the upper elevations. This is also the season of flash floods in the desert.

Accommodations

Arizona visitors should experience no difficulty in finding suitable accommodations along the major highways. The principal routes are dotted with excellent hotels, motels, resorts, and trailer parks, particularly near the larger cities and towns. Reservations are essential during busy seasons in popular tourist areas such as Grand Canyon National Park, and they're advisable as a general rule anywhere.

(Continued on next page)

Since many of the Arizona resorts operate on a seasonal basis, you are likely to find some resorts in the northern part of the state closed during the winter and some of those in the south closed during the summer. Many motels and hotels stay open all year, offering off-season rates.

Dude ranches

Arizona's specialty—the dude ranch—is a big desert ranch that makes a special play for winter guests. Some provide tutors or are near community schools so that guests' children can keep up with their school work during an extended stay. Emphasis is on comfort—and sometimes on luxury. Clusters of such ranches have sprung up around Wickenburg, Phoenix, and Tucson. Around Sedona, in the Verde country, and scattered elsewhere at higher elevations around the state, you'll find ranches that generally conform to the more usual summer-season pattern.

Camping

Campgrounds are generally equipped with fireplaces, picnic tables, garbage pits, and sanitary facilities. Not all have water. For a complete guide to Arizona's campgrounds, see Sunset's *Western Campsites*, updated annually.

Desert camping. The main problems involved in desert camping revolve around the desert's unpredictability—strong and sudden winds, wide fluctuations in temperature, and limited sources of food, water, and fuel. The best months for desert camping are from November to April. The spring months (late February to early April) are the most popular because of the possibility of seeing the desert in bloom. January and February nights are cold, but the days are usually clear and warm. Spring and fall days range from warm to hot; the nights are usually cool.

Do not set up your camp in a dry wash. In summer and early fall these washes are avenues for flash floods.

For most desert campers, a tent is not enough, you need some type of windbreak to protect sitting and cooking areas.

With few exceptions, you will have to take your own water and fuel supply. Winds can make cooking over a campfire impossible; for this reason, most desert campers use a gasoline stove. Food does not keep well in the desert, so

you will have to depend for the most part on canned and dried items.

Sunburn lotion, a large canteen of water, and a first-aid kit are essentials if you go hiking.

These rules of hiking are extremely important in the desert: 1) Before you wander off, tell someone where you are heading and when you expect to return. 2) Look for landmarks along the way to aid you in retracing the trail. 3) Don't hike alone.

Indian reservations

Visitors are welcome on the Indian reservations, but anyone visiting a reservation should bear in mind at all times that he is a guest on the Indians' land and should act accordingly.

The Indians are usually willing to pose for photographs, but they consider this a service to the visitor and expect to be paid for it. Ask permission before taking a photograph of an Indian or his family.

Because most Indian ceremonies are of a religious nature, photographing them is generally prohibited. Some of the Indian ceremonial dances are never performed in public; some are performed before only a limited number of spectators. An admission fee is usually charged.

Hunting and fishing

Deer are found in most of the forested areas of Arizona. In addition, some parts of the state have elk, antelope, black bears, javelinas (peccaries), wild turkeys, bighorn sheep, and a considerable number of wildcats, coyotes, and mountain lions.

The national forests in Arizona contain many popular fishing lakes and about 500 miles of trout streams. The Colorado River offers several hundred miles of fishing water. Game fish include the largemouthed black bass, crappie, trout, and channel catfish. Havasu Lake, Lake Mead, and Lake Powell are the most popular and heavily fished waters along the rivers. The waters below Hoover Dam and Davis Dam are popular for rainbow trout fishing.

A valid Arizona fishing license is required for all fishing. Persons fishing from a boat on the waters that border neighboring states must have a valid license from either state and a special use stamp from the other.

On about half of Arizona's lakes, gasoline-powered outboard motors are prohibited, although electric trolling motors may be allowed; check before you launch your motorboat.

You'll find details of these sports in each section of this book.

For more information on hunting or fishing, write to the Arizona Game and Fish Department, 2222 W. Greenway Road, Phoenix, AZ 85023.

Skiing

Arizona has some excellent ski areas. The Arizona Snow Bowl, on the slopes of San Francisco Peaks 14 miles northeast of Flagstaff, is the best developed ski area in the state. Other ski areas include Mount Lemmon, 40 miles northeast of Tucson; Bill Williams Mountain, 4 miles south of Williams; and Sunrise Park, in the White Mountains on the Fort Apache Indian Reservation, owned and operated by the Apaches. Each of these areas has slopes to accommodate the beginning as well as the expert skier. Mount Lemmon also has some excellent cross-country trails.

Driving tips

Because of the wide range of climate, driving conditions vary accordingly, but there are some things to be aware of wherever you are.

Gasoline. Throughout Arizona, outside of the main metropolitan areas, service stations may be many miles apart, even along major roads. Fill up your tank when you start out and when you can along your route.

Water. The same applies to water: check your radiator, and carry three or more gallons of extra water if you're crossing the desert (even on a freeway) or venturing off the main roads.

Dirt and gravel roads. Much of Arizona is still served by unpaved roads (and many of the people living in the back country drive pickups or four-wheel-drive vehicles). In the mountains and highlands, many side roads mentioned in this book are closed by winter snows and are too muddy during spring thaws and after summer thunderstorms. It's best to plan these trips for summer or early fall. In wet weather, be prepared with chains. At all times, if you're exploring the back roads, it's a good idea to carry a tow rope, shovel, tire pump, air pressure gauge, reliable flashlight, and some gunny sacks for traction in slush or sand.

Livestock. When driving through open range, watch out for cattle or sheep. Slow down when you approach a rise or a blind curve; there may be sheep or cattle in the road.

In the desert. Desert driving, too, has its own characteristic kinks that become second nature to Arizona drivers.

Sand. If you get stuck in the sand, don't spin the wheels. Deflate the tires to 15 pounds and spread those gunny sacks in front of the wheels, tucking them in under the tires. Pull out slowly in low gear. Once you get back on a hard surface, pump up your tires again or drive slowly to the next service station. Soft tires overheat and can blow out at high speed. Best advice: if the road looks questionable, don't try it.

Air pressure. Carry a low-pressure tire gauge in your car and check the pressure from time to time if you drive for long distances in hot weather. If the pressure increases alarmingly, do not release air. Pull off the road and let the tires cool off. Releasing air will simply make them underinflated when they cool.

Sandstorms. Wind-driven sand can seriously damage a car. In addition to pitting the windshield and scouring off paint, sand can work its way into the engine through the air cleaner and damage the moving parts. If you encounter a driving sandstorm—one with heavy wind that forces sand into the car even with the windows shut—stop at the nearest roadside rest. If a rest area isn't available, pull off as far as possible, turn off your lights (so as not to mislead other drivers), and try to seek shelter away from your car. As soon as the storm has passed, stop at a service station and have the oil, carburetor, and air filter checked for grit.

Flash floods. Along the roads that dip into washes in the desert and foothills, you may encounter signs warning of "flash flood area." The summer thunderstorms that quickly dump inches of rain into the mountains and hills can fill those dry washes with rushing, silt-laden water—bank to bank. Be aware of this if you're driving during the summer storm season. A flash flood may fill the wash ahead of you even though the cloudburst may be out of sight behind a ridge.

Breakdowns. If your car breaks down leaving you stranded, especially on a desert road, stay with your car and out of the sunlight as much as possible and wait for help.

If you're on a very remote road, and must walk for help, wait until dark and insist that your family stay with the car. Take some water with you (it's always good to carry water in more than one container); leave enough for the people staying behind. Go back the same way you came, and don't try short-cuts.

The Grand Canyon

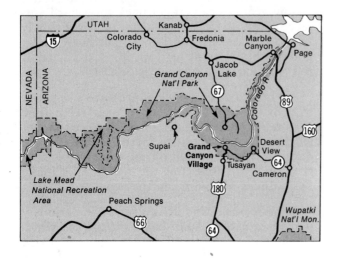

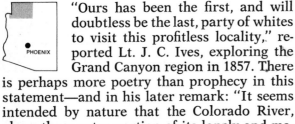

miles apart as the crow flies, are nevertheless separated by a 215-mile drive.

When visitors speak of the park, they are usually referring to the South Rim and the year-round tourist facilities concentrated in bustling Grand Canyon Village. The higher North Rim, directly across the canyon, is covered by heavy snows in winter. Accommodations, also comfortable and attractive, are fewer, and facilities are somewhat scaled down in comparison with those of the South Rim. It's the favorite of those who prefer less elbow-rubbing and less bustle—and those who have seen the canyon from the South Rim.

THE SOUTH RIM

The South Rim of the Grand Canyon is enjoyable year-round, although there are seasonal changes at its 7,000-foot altitude. Each season brings a new setting to this magnificent natural stage. From June to September daytime temperatures reach into the 80s or 90s with cool 40-degree temperatures at night. The warm sun, especially at sunrise and sunset, highlights the rustic colors of the upper canyon walls and grounds; these colors contrast sharply with the dark shadows that reach deep down to the canyon floor. Sudden thunderstorms and turbulent skies frequently surprise the canyon in July and August, setting a different mood—a favorite one of many photographers.

Autumn is brief, with clear days. First snow falls in October or November. From the first permanent snowfall into April, nights may be frosty, but daytime temperatures are in the 40s and 50s.

If you're approaching from the west on U.S. 66, turn north on Arizona Highway 64 at Williams. The drive to the park is a pleasant 60 miles through rolling hills covered at lower elevations with bunch grass, junipers, and desert shrubs, then with Ponderosa pine forest near Tusayan, a growing community just south of the park boundary.

From Flagstaff there are two ways to reach the canyon. U.S. Highway 180 angles northwest out of the city on the west side of the San Fran-

"Ours has been the first, and will doubtless be the last, party of whites to visit this profitless locality," reported Lt. J. C. Ives, exploring the Grand Canyon region in 1857. There is perhaps more poetry than prophecy in this statement—and in his later remark: "It seems intended by nature that the Colorado River, along the greater portion of its lonely and majestic way, shall be forever unvisited and undisturbed."

Since Ives' time, the Grand Canyon has been the abode of ranchers, miners, prospectors, horse thieves, hermits, and bootleggers. Around the turn of the century, its vastness was laced with an ambitious network of good trails. There were hotels, tourist camps, orchards, and gardens at various levels all the way down to the river, and several cable cars across it. But the canyon triumphed. The resorts petered out, cable cars rusted in their moorings, and neglected trails disappeared. Today you look out over a Grand Canyon where maintained trails are few and the only human habitations are the hidden ancestral home of the Havasupai Indians and a few tiny green oases like Phantom Ranch.

For 277 river miles, the Colorado passes through Grand Canyon National Park. It divides the park so that the tourist areas of the North Rim and South Rim, although only 11

BRILLIANT COLORS intensify the well-defined shapes of the Grand Canyon and emphasize the overwhelming scale of the gorge. The view changes with time of day and kind of weather.

THE NORTH RIM supports great forests of aspen, royal oak, and conifers. At 8,000 feet, fall color arrives earlier here than on the opposite rim, which is 1,000 feet lower.

cisco Peaks, meeting Arizona 64 about 30 miles south of Grand Canyon Village.

A second route also takes you north from Flagstaff on U.S. 89 almost to Cameron on the Navajo reservation. There you turn west on Arizona 64 and enter the park near the eastern-most development at Desert View.

If you prefer to fly to the South Rim, there's regular scheduled airline service to the Grand Canyon National Park Airport from Las Vegas and Phoenix, with bus service to Grand Canyon Village. Transcontinental bus lines serve Flagstaff and Williams, and there are bus lines from both towns to the village. A regional airline serves Flagstaff.

The AMTRAK railroad goes to Flagstaff; from there you can take a bus.

Where to stay

Park lodging facilities have a combined 770 rooms, but during the busy season from Easter Week to after Labor Day, the South Rim is crowded by many more visitors than those facilities will accommodate. During this rush, you must have reservations or, as many visitors do, stay at a motel or lodge at Tusayan, Flagstaff, Williams, or Cameron. You can camp at one of two campgrounds in the park, or two campgrounds near Tusayan. From November to April, there's plenty of room, but reserve for holidays. Trailer space in the park also must be reserved.

In the Village. The Grand Canyon National Park Lodges, South Rim concessionaire, operates all accommodations on the South Rim except the Park Service campgrounds. For information and reservations, write them at Grand Canyon, AZ 86023, or telephone (602) 638-2401.

El Tovar Hotel, built in 1904 of native stone and rough-hewn pine logs, is the patriarch of the South Rim and one of the famous hostelries of the nation. Rates are comparable to those of metropolitan motels. Open all year.

Bright Angel Lodge, offering both lodge rooms and cabins, is the center of busy-season activity. It's open during spring, summer, and fall.

Thunderbird and Kachina Lodges, between El Tovar Hotel and Bright Angel Lodge on the rim, are modern facilities featuring deluxe, up-to-date rooms and suites. Open all year.

Yavapai Lodge, back from the rim in the woods near the visitor center, is a modern lodge-motel, open March to November. The large cafeteria here serves three meals a day.

The Trailer Village has 106 sites with cold water and electricity and sewage hookups. It's open all year but there's a 7-day limit May 1 to October 21. Trailer spaces must be reserved. There is a fee.

The Grand Canyon Motor Lodge offers motel rooms and cabins and the lowest rates. It has a cafeteria serving three meals a day. Open from July to September.

Outside the Village. Just south of the park entrance on U.S. 180 is the Moqui Lodge motel and restaurant. At Tusayan, just south of Moqui, are additional large motels. The old hotel at Cameron, on the bank of the Little Colorado, also offers comfortable accommodations in just over an hour's drive from Grand Canyon Village.

Camping. There are two Park Service campgrounds on the South Rim, one in Grand Canyon Village and a smaller one at Desert View. The Mather Campground, in the forested village south of the visitor center, has 329 campsites and piped water. At the nearby Camper Service Building are showers, laundromat, and ice (April to October). The big general store has groceries and supplies.

Just south of Tusayan, the Forest Service Ten-X Campground has 70 campsites with trailer parking. Facilities include toilets but no trailer hookups. Bring your own drinking water. It's open April to November; you can stay 14 days. There is also a privately operated campground near Tusayan.

At Desert View at the east end of the park is another Park Service campground with 50 campsites, piped drinking water, but no trailer hookups. There is a small fee; admission is on a first-come basis, with a 7-day limit. It's open from about mid-May to October, depending upon the weather.

Getting around

Grand Canyon Village is strung out for about a mile and a half through the forest of the South Rim, a dumbbell-shaped development with clusters of facilities at each end. Connecting them is the ¾-mile paved road through the forest—vehicle traffic sometimes is heavy—and the nature trail along the rim, part of a 4-mile rim trail.

You can visit everything in the village on foot without exertion. Beyond it, however, the West Rim Drive to the view point at Hermit's Rest is 8 miles, and the East Rim Drive out to spectacular Desert View is 27 miles. Shuttle bus service provides transportation around the village, as far east as the Yavapai Museum, and along the West Rim Drive from about Memorial Day through Labor Day. During that period private autos are not allowed on the West Rim Drive.

Auto rentals. You can arrange for an auto rental or a chauffeur-driven van at the Transportation Desk in the Bright Angel Lodge and at El Tovar. You also can rent cars at Grand Canyon Airport.

Bus tours. A tour of the West Rim Drive stops at Trail View (overlooking Bright Angel Trail into the canyon), Hopi and Pima points, and Hermit's Rest. The East Rim tour goes to Desert View, with stops at Lipan Point, Moran Point, and the Yavapai Museum.

Flying into the canyon. You can make a flying tour of the canyon from the Grand Canyon Airport at Tusayan, or from Williams, Page, or Las Vegas. Helicopter tours leave from Tusayan. Get information at transportation desks, the visitor center, or the airports mentioned; or telephone (800) 228-2200.

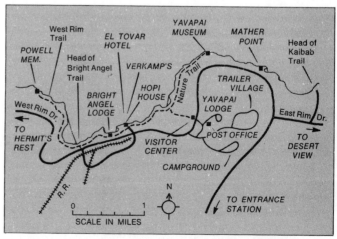

SOUTH RIM abounds in attractions, view points.

As you stand at the edge of the Grand Canyon and gaze down the neatly stratified rocks into the depths of the canyon, you're looking back some twenty million centuries. When you descend into the canyon, you pass through many of the major climates found in North America; you'll see a bewildering variety of plants and animals that, outside this canyon, would probably need to spread out over a continent to find a suitable environment.

The birth of a canyon. The erosive forces that created this enormous cleft in the earth's crust are the same as those that carve a roadside gully. In the beginning, a quiet river flowed through a gently sloping plain. The river began running faster, cutting a deeper track, as pressures from within the earth slowly tilted the surface. The deepening chan-nel caused land on both sides to erode into the river, creating an ever-widening V-shaped canyon.

A chronicle of time. The canyon today exposes a wealth of earth history; the story is written in neatly deposited layers used by geologists as a primer. Among the rock of the inner gorge is the oldest man has seen exposed on this planet—two billion years old.

Walking a continent. In a hike to the bottom of the canyon and out again you would experience a variation in climate and plant and animal life ranging from that of Mexico's Sonora Desert to Canada's Hudson Bay, from the blazing heat, the yucca, and the spiny lizards of the low-desert bottom to the sub-arctic blue spruce at the top of the canyon.

Viewing the canyon

Along the South Rim are many splendid view points. Each has its own characteristics, no one point giving you a complete view. Then, too, the canyon scene changes constantly as the sun crosses the sky, shadows move down in the depths, and haze softens the light.

Mather Point. As the main road into Grand Canyon Village from the south entrance (U.S. 180) swings west toward the village, it approaches the rim of the canyon at Mather Point. This is where most visitors get their first glimpse of the canyon. For different outlooks, try the East Rim Drive, which intersects with State 64, ¾ of a mile south of Mather Point.

Along the East Rim Drive. Five more major vista points are spotted between the intersection and Desert View, as well as several "wall stops" where the road approaches the rim. Yaki Point, about a mile on the road west from the intersection, juts out into the canyon and offers views over a 200-degree arc. Three miles east of Yaki Point is the trail down a hill to Duck-on-the-Rock, a curious, much-photographed formation with views northeastward. Grandview Point, another 5 miles east, affords another view northeastward and a look at a good stretch of the river itself. Moran Point, 6 miles east of Grandview, offers broad views westward and is a late-afternoon favorite. From here you can see the white water of Hance Rapids in the river below. Lipan Point, another 5 miles east, is considered by many the most beautiful South Rim overlook. Because this and the next two points are in the bend of the river, you can see back up the river. Navajo Point, a mile east and close to Desert View, offers another scenic vista.

Desert View. If you approach the Grand Canyon from the east on State 64 (from Cameron), this will be your first view into the canyon. For many visitors, this is a favorite. From here you look both ways from the apex of a right-angle bend in the canyon—north to the notch where the Little Colorado enters, and west toward the South Rim promontories. Here, too, is a 70-foot watchtower, built of native stone on a steel frame. The glass-enclosed observatory top is the highest point on the South Rim.

Along the Rim Trail. There is a more or less continuous trail along the rim from Mather Point to Hermit's Rest. It is paved from Yavapai Point to Maricopa Point. The trail is one long view path, although there are specific overlook points. At the east end, about a mile and a half from the Lodge, is Yavapai Point, offering broad views up and down stream. In the Yavapai Museum, the park provides exhibits that describe various geologic formations in the canyon. Just west is Grandeur Point, with a slightly more westerly view. West of the Lodge, on the West Rim Trail, you can walk to Maricopa Point for more views across the canyon and back to the east. Here the trail ends, and you hike, bike, or ride shuttle buses eight miles along the West Rim Drive to Hermit's Rest (see The West Rim Drive, below). Rental bikes are available at Maricopa Point and Hermit's Rest.

The West Rim Drive. West of Maricopa Point, the Powell Memorial commemorates explorer Major John Wesley Powell, who led the first boat party down the river and made the first geological survey of the canyon. Just west of it is Hopi Point and the best views from the West Rim Drive. From Mojave Point, less than a mile west, you also have fine sunset views. From Pima Point, 3½ miles further west, you may hear the roar of the rapids, visible below. The drive is closed to private autos from mid-April through Labor Day. Shuttle buses leave every 15 minutes from below the Bright Angel Lodge parking lot, stopping at each view point. The round trip takes about three hours, but most visitors stop off and walk around the view points and catch a later bus. You can cover all the view points in half a day.

Hermit's Rest. At the end of the drive is Hermit's Rest, the little building erected in 1914 around a huge stone fireplace, at the head of the Hermit Trail. There are restrooms here.

Nature Trail. The ¾ of a mile of Rim Trail east of the village to the turnoff to the visitor center, and the ½ mile to the center, are a nature trail of marked stations keyed to a guide book available at the center or at the trail heads. The book describes and explains botanical specimens, evidences of the canyon's geologic history, and aspects of its ecology.

Other points of interest

To understand the geology, ecology, and human history of the Grand Canyon, you should take advantage of the fine exhibits and educational programs offered by the National Park Service, particularly at the visitor center, the Yavapai Museum, and the Tusayan ruins and museum. There also are commercial establishments which can add to your enjoyment of this unique area.

Visitor center. At the park headquarters' visitor center you can see exhibits of the geologic history and formation of the canyon. A collection of original river-running boats from the earliest trips is on display, and you can watch a demonstration of Navajo Indian rug weaving. In the courtyard you'll find samples of the various kinds of boats used in running the river. You can purchase books, pamphlets, and maps. The Park Service offers information on geology, life zones, habitation by man, and hiking and camping in the canyon.

Yavapai Museum. In the small stone building at Yavapai Point, you'll find a glass-enclosed viewing room and exhibits on the geologic history of the canyon. There may be special programs by park rangers; check the park newspaper, the *Grand Canyon Guide*, for schedules or inquire at the museum or visitor center. The museum is open 11 to 5 daily and also from 7 to 9 p.m. in the summer.

Tusayan Ruins and Museum. Just south of the East Rim Drive, about 4 miles east of Moran Point, are the ruins of a small Indian village about 800 years old. A cluster of low, stone walls among the trees outlines the Pueblo-type houses and a kiva. The small museum offers descriptions of their Indian culture and exhibits objects recovered during the 1930 excavation.

Into the depths

You really haven't felt the impact of the Grand Canyon until you've seen it from the bottom. The awesome one-mile depth suddenly becomes a reality. On the South Rim you're in the cool Transition life zone of predominantly Ponderosa pine forests. On the canyon floor, you're in the Lower Sonoran life zone, the Sonora desert of cactus and yucca, populated by lizards, rattlesnakes, and other desert animals. Summer temperatures can top 120°.

From the South Rim you can ride a mule all the way to the bottom or hike in and stay overnight at Phantom Ranch or the campgrounds.

By mule. Every day, weather permitting, all year long, the famous mule trains plod in and out of the depths. To ride the mule train you have to be in good physical condition, over 12 years old, and under 200 pounds fully dressed and equipped. There are no exceptions. Riders are required to sign a liability release.

This is not a trip for people who fear heights. At many points sheer rock walls drop hundreds of feet from the trail's edge. It's not unusual for acrophobia vicitms to dismount at the first stopping point and hike a mile back up to the rim. By then it's too late for a refund.

The one-day, 12-mile round trip on the Bright Angel Trail takes you down to the Tonto Plateau overlooking the Inner Gorge, about two-thirds of the total descent.

The two-day trip to Phantom Ranch goes down the same trail but returns up the steeper South Kaibab Trail. Overnight accommodations are at Phantom Ranch, the rustic resort on Bright Angel Creek.

Rates for the trip include mule, guide, box lunch on the trail, cabin (single occupancy), dinner, and breakfast. Up to four riders may share a cabin and save.

You can get complete information by writing to Grand Canyon National Park Lodges, Grand Canyon, AZ 86023, or phoning (602) 638-2401, or at the transportation desks. Reserve as early as possible—at least six months ahead for summer mule trips. You may include a deposit, but acceptance isn't final until you appear, obviously old enough and in good health, and "weigh in."

Hiking in. You can make short day hikes to points on the Bright Angel or Kaibab trails, or hike all the way down to overnight accommodations at Phantom Ranch, or you can camp at free campgrounds on the main trails (see Overnighting for hikers). Rangers rate the 16-mile round trip to the river as "an exhausting hike,"

even for experienced hikers and do not recommend it as a one-day hike. The Park Service recommends carrying one gallon of water per person per day.

If fatigue stops you or you have an accident on the trail and have to be rescued by mule, it's expensive. There are emergency telephones on Bright Angel and Kaibab trails.

Overnighting for hikers. You can stay at the Phantom Ranch (if you have reservations) at the same rates for rooms and meals as paid by the mule-riders. There's also a dormitory.

There are free campgrounds near Phantom Ranch, at Indian Gardens on the Bright Angel Trail, and at Cottonwood and Roaring Springs on the North Kaibab Trail to the North Rim. However, camping spaces must be reserved and all campers must have permit tags, obtainable at the visitor center desk. For information or reservations, write Back-country Reservations Office, Grand Canyon National Park, AZ 86023, or phone (602) 638-2474.

THE NORTH RIM

On the North Rim, where the elevation is a thousand feet or so higher than on the South Rim, snow falls early and deep. Early October is the time when the North Rim is most colorful, with groves of golden aspens (absent from the pine-and-juniper woods of the South Rim) shining out against shadowy blue curtains of tall spruces and firs that make up much of the forest cover of the Kaibab Plateau.

Because of the higher elevation and heavy snow, roads and concessions are closed during the winter.

Actual closing of the North Rim entrance road is determined by snowfall. Indian summer may last into November—or the road may be closed temporarily by a mid-October storm, only to dry off and remain not only passable but warmly inviting until late November.

The common approach to the North Rim from Arizona is north from Flagstaff on U.S. 89 to Bitter Springs, then north and west on U.S. 89A to the turnoff of State 67 at Jacob Lake. From the north, the nearest major highways are Interstate 15 near St. George and U.S. 89 from Salt Lake City.

From Jacob Lake, it's 32 miles to the park entrance (there's no gas station between Jacob Lake and Kaibab Lodge just outside the park) and another 13 miles to the rim. It's a scenic

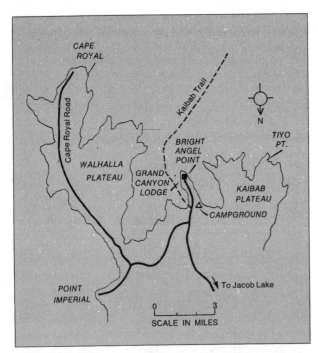

NORTH RIM is more remote, quieter than South

drive, up the gradually-tilted Kaibab Plateau, climbing to above 8,800 feet before descending to the rim. You can take a bus from Cedar City, Utah, during June, July, and August.

Where to stay

Compared to the South Rim, accommodations are few on the North Rim. From mid-May to October, Grand Canyon Lodge offers rustic cabin accommodations. For reservations, contact TWA Services, Inc., 4045 S. Spencer Street, Las Vegas, Nevada 89109.

Outside the park, motel accommodations are available at Kaibab Lodge, 5 miles north of the North Rim entrance station, and at Jacob Lake, 32 miles north of the entrance station.

Camping. Bright Angel Campground is the only close-in campground on the North Rim—78 improved sites in a quiet, wooded spot sprinkled with aspen leaves, and only a short distance from store and cafeteria. Water and firewood are available. There is a small fee, and the limit is 7 days. There are no trailer utility hookups.

Camping is not allowed elsewhere in the park, but there's a smaller Forest Service improved campground at De Motte on State 67, just north of the park boundary, and campgrounds at Jacob Lake.

Another view

The higher, more imposing North Rim offers a totally different view of the canyon. Nature's intricate engineering of this enormous channel is much more apparent here—providing deep side canyons, free-standing islands of rock reaching up from the canyon floor, and narrow promontories that intrude into the canyon. During much of the year, as the sun is inclined toward the south, the opposite South Rim reflects a more somber mood as its walls are darkened by long shadows.

Four major view points dot the North Rim:

Bright Angel Point. The tip of this promontory is a ⅜-mile walk from the road where you'll get your first look into the canyon. Below it, on the east, is the trail down to the Phantom Ranch

COLORFUL LEAVES of Rocky Mountain maple arch over hikers (above) exploring upper portion of the 21-mile Kaibab Trail. A thick grove of aspens (left) on the North Rim provides shelter for mule deer.

and the river. This is also the site of Grand Canyon Lodge.

Cape Royal. Here is the southernmost point on the North Rim, jutting out into the big bend of the canyon. From here, and from Angel's Window (a gaping hole punctured through a narrow promontory by the endless force of wind and frost) less than a mile north, you can look across the north-south gorge to the Painted Desert. It's 26 miles from Bright Angel Point on a paved road.

Point Imperial. This high point, at 8,800 feet, is the northernmost roadside viewpoint, overlooking the beginning of the Grand Canyon where the Colorado River emerges from narrow Marble Gorge. It's three miles off the Cape Royal road on an eastward turnoff about 5½ miles from Grand Canyon Lodge.

During your stay, enjoy the luxury of taking a whole day to drive 67 miles—the combined round-trip distance to Point Imperial and Cape Royal. Take lunch and water along and just dawdle. On the Walhalla Plateau you can follow a primitive road through the aspens if the ground is dry.

Point Sublime. From this point, you get the westernmost view of either side, and you see the narrowest opening between the two rims. To reach Point Sublime, go back north on the highway almost to the park entrance. A primitive road turns off and goes 17 miles through pine and aspen groves to the point. The road's not always open, so inquire at the ranger station or the information desk in the lodge.

Getting around

If you're not driving a car, you can still see the highlights of the North Rim (except Point Sublime) by doing a little hiking, horseback riding, or taking the single but substantial bus tour.

Hikes. Along the rim between the Lodge and Bright Angel Campground is the gentle, 1½-

AN INCREDIBLE SUNSET paints the canyon walls. As far as the eye can see, stark silhouettes of canyon formations stretch out in a vast, unforgettable view.

mile Transept Canyon Trail. The Uncle Jim Trail starts at the Kaibab Trail parking lot, a mile north of the campground, and takes you 3 miles through the trees to an overlook above the trail and the main canyon. The Widforss Trail is a 10-mile round trip through forestland to a canyon overlook from the next promontory west of Bright Angel Point. Ken Patrick Trail winds for 12 miles through the forest and along the rim from Point Imperial to the North Kaibab trailhead.

Trail riding. You can take a guided 3-hour horseback trip to Uncle Jim's Point, and other rim rides may be available by arrangement, but only sure-footed mules go down the North Kaibab Trail.

By bus. Although there's only one bus tour, you shouldn't miss it unless you're going to drive the same route. That's the bus trip every afternoon to both Cape Royal and Point Imperial.

An interpretive program. Even if you're not on the bus tour, you can join the bus group at Cape Royal for the ranger's talk. There are campfire programs nightly next to Bright Angel Campground and illustrated presentations at the Grand Canyon Lodge, usually with some entertainment included. During the summer rangers conduct nature walks and other special programs. Check the *Grand Canyon Guide* for schedules.

Into the canyon

From the North Rim you can go into the canyon depths down to the river and back by mule or by hiking in. It's tougher here than from the South Rim; you start from almost 1,000 feet higher up. You can make a 9-mile, 1-day mule trek to Roaring Springs and back, and there's a shorter mule ride along the rim, 3½ miles round trip. You also can make the trip to Phantom Ranch, similar to that from the South Rim and at comparable rates, if the party has 3 or more riders. These trips must be reserved.

FOR CANYON EXPLORERS, the depths offer challenges, surprises, and impressive scenery. From either rim, you can hike down or ride a mule. Boat tours are many and varied. They take adventurers through quiet water and pounding rapids and combine canyon viewing from the river with free time for recreation ashore.

Write to Grand Canyon Scenic Rides, Kanab, Utah 84741.

Hiking in. If you're rugged, you can hike down the North Kaibab Trail. It's 14 miles one way, and the Park Service recommends you break it up with an overnight rest at one of the two inner-canyon campgrounds. It's even more rugged coming back up; you climb 5,800 feet in that 14 miles. Ask for hiking information at the ranger station.

Tuweep area

Confirmed back-country probers are discovering the breathtaking vistas of the Tuweep area, its breezy, uncluttered campground, and its spectacular lava flows.

You can reach this region by turning south from State 389 on the Kaibab Indian Reservation, west of Fredonia, near Pipe Springs National Monument (see North of the Canyon, page 20). The unpaved roads, unsuitable for passenger cars in wet weather, are almost a guarantee of solitude. It's 65 miles on graded road from Fredonia to the Tuweep Ranger Station and another 5 miles on unimproved road to Toroweap Point, the awesome overlook of a sheer drop of 3,000 feet to the river.

There are a few ranches along the way, but you cannot count on finding gasoline even in an emergency. Fill your tank just before you go, carry an extra supply in a safe jerry can, and carry water.

Toroweap Overlook. Your approach is through a wide break in the plateau, called Toroweap Valley. At the end of the valley, ahead of you and right on the lip of the gorge, is a unique landmark in a land of flat-topped mesas and abrupt rimrocks—a smoothly-rounded, sagebrush-dotted pile of volcanic cinders called Vulcan's Throne.

Looking upstream, you see the Grand Canyon of geometrical, sedimentary ledges and cliffs and talus slopes. Downstream, for mile after mile, thick lava flows form steep dark deltas over ridges and gullies or hang like frozen black waterfalls on the cliffs.

Far below you, the floods of the river have undercut, exposed, and polished a glittering black embroidery of columnar basalt bending every which way. Directly across the chasm, Prospect Wash has furnished you a cross-section diagram by slicing its deep canyon right through a cinder cone.

Here, if you have brought water, you can camp in the shelter of piñon pines and low rock outcrops; there are two campsites with tables and stoves. If the wind blows (or the space is taken), you can go back a mile, turn off the main road at the rustic rest rooms, and go on a few yards to another campground in the lee of a sandstone overhang.

NORTH OF THE CANYON

On the north side of the Grand Canyon in Arizona's northwest corner is the Arizona Strip, a stretch of land about 50 by 140 miles, separated from the rest of the state by the Colorado River. It was settled by early Mormons who moved down from Utah, and because of the great barrier formed by the Grand Canyon, it is historically and culturally linked more closely to Utah than to Arizona.

Much of the region is grassland or sparsely forested with piñon, juniper, cottonwood, and willow; but the Mount Trumbull Division of the Kaibab National Forest, southwest of Fredonia, contains more than 4,000 acres of Ponderosa pines.

From the north, roads lead into this corner of Arizona from St. George and Kanab, Utah. From the east and south, you can reach the area on U.S. 89A via Marble Canyon (Navajo Bridge) and Jacob Lake. There are lodges, motels, and hotels in St. George, Kanab, and Fredonia, and an inn at Jacob Lake.

Marble Canyon

Entrance to the Arizona Strip from the east is dramatic; the slender, shining steel arch and deck of Navajo Bridge spanning 616 feet across the gorge, 467 feet above the river, look breathtakingly fragile. Cliffs rise to 800 feet in some parts of the gorge, the redwall limestone making this stretch of water a favorite of river-running photographers.

It's only by boat or raft that you'll see the inner secrets of this colorful canyon. The river runners start at Lee's Ferry, 4 miles north of the bridge on the west, where the Paria River meets the Colorado. Here you will find a motel, stores, service station, and boat rentals and supplies. It's a favorite fishing spot.

Paria Canyon

Lee's Ferry is the eastern entrance to the Paria Canyon Primitive Area, a narrow, sinuous chasm slicing 40 miles northwest from the Colorado River. It's for hikers only, and once you enter the narrow canyon vault, with vertical walls soaring to 1,200 feet, you go all the way or turn around and go back; there's no other way out. It's a 5-day trek from end to end. Of course, you can take a short day-hike as far as you want. Be prepared to wade at several points.

Permits are required. They are obtainable at no cost from the U.S. Bureau of Land Management, 320 North 1st East, Kanab, Utah 84741, or from the ranger at the White House entrance.

Start your hike at the upstream end, just downstream from where U.S. 89 crosses the Paria River in Utah, about 55 miles west of Glen Canyon City. Check in at the ranger station to be sure water conditions are safe before entering the narrows, where flash flood hazards are dangerous, especially during July, August, and September.

For a detailed brochure on Paria Canyon, write to the Bureau of Land Management at the above address in Kanab or at 3204 Federal Building, 230 N. First Avenue, Phoenix, AZ 85025.

House Rock Valley Buffalo Range

As you go west from Navajo Bridge toward the Kaibab Plateau, you come to a sign pointing south into the House Rock Valley Buffalo Range. In this area between the Kaibab high country and the desert rim of the Grand Canyon, bison roam free.

After an easy 21-mile drive south on a good dirt road, you arrive at Buffalo Ranch, the refuge headquarters, where the supervisor will answer your questions and tell you where you might be able to see buffalo in some of the nearby draws.

Onto the Kaibab Plateau

Ordinarily, people take the two-thirds of the Kaibab Plateau that is national forest land as a mere prologue to the one-third that is in Grand Canyon National Park. Actually, the national forest is a wonderful region in which to camp in solitude and study wildlife—and it has roads to more points on the Grand Canyon's North Rim than you find inside the national park.

For serene, enticing views of the Grand Canyon, two of the more rewarding drives are to Crazy Jug Point—on forest roads 1 and 1A from Big Springs or De Motte Campground and

RUNNING THE COLORADO

"We are swept broadside down, and are prevented, by the rebounding waters, from striking against the wall . . . We toss about . . . in these billows, and are carried past the danger." These are the recorded words of John Wesley Powell, a one-armed, ex-artillery major, describing the first known boat ride down the turbulent, often violent, Colorado River of 1869. In that year the major took a small party in four boats to run the length of the Green and the Colorado rivers to the bottom of the Grand Canyon. Losing two of his boats and three men left the party unnerved.

Things have changed since that early river-run. Today's boats are much better equipped to take the pounding rapids, and the river's raging water is somewhat more tranquil now. But running the Colorado—still exciting—is one of the best ways to study the river and the canyons.

Tours down the Colorado are many and varied. With some you'll be part of a large group running the river in the big nylon and neoprene pontoon-type rafts, or you can choose a tour that uses the smaller, more maneuverable wooden dories. Boats and rafts are powered by motor or oars. The latter is likely to give you a ride closer to what Major Powell must have experienced. Almost all crafts used are compartmentalized making them virtually unsinkable.

Safety is a primary consideration on the tours. The boatmen-guides are all veteran river runners, skilled in the rapids and well-informed about the sights. Meals, usually cooked by the boatmen, are included.

Basic equipment is normally provided: a life jacket and a waterproof bag to hold your sleeping bag and clothing. Tour operators will supply you with equipment lists.

Itineraries for the tours are carefully planned to include hiking and exploring the river banks and canyons along the way. Most tours will allow you to run all the rapids, although you may prefer to pass on a few and walk along the bank. Though it is a rare occurrence, boats can be upset in the rapids.

Reservations for the 4 to 20-day trips should be made early (as much as a year in advance if possible) to get your preferred time and type of tour. Write to National Park Service, South Rim, Grand Canyon National Park, Grand Canyon, AZ 86023, for tour listings and information. There's also a one-day river trip —five hours of smooth-water drifting from Page to Lee's Ferry, with bus service. Inquire at South Rim and North Rim tour desks.

through Big Saddle Hunting Camp, all on maintained road; and to Timp Point (prettiest approach is Quaking Aspen Canyon—the last part "primitive" but not difficult).

There are marshes and mud on the Kaibab, but no perennial streams and little surface water of any kind—just a few springs piped into stock tanks, and some small ponds and shallow sink holes called "lakes"—so carry your own water supply. Jacob Lake and Kaibab Lodge are the only places where you can buy gasoline (outside the national park), so don't let your tank run low on a back-country trip. Always expect to get stuck in the mud and equip yourself accordingly.

Among Ponderosa pines—not so much among the firs and spruces of the really high country along State 67—you may catch a glimpse of the spectacular white-tailed Kaibab squirrel, a species found nowhere in the world except on the Kaibab Plateau. This is also the summer range of the Kaibab deer herd, and frequently you can see deer from the highway.

Although you may camp almost anywhere you like on the Kaibab, aside from the campground at Jacob Lake and De Motte Campground, the only "improvements" you're likely to encounter are crude hitching rails and shaky tables left by other campers.

Pipe Spring National Monument

The monument, in the Kaibab Indian Reservation near the Utah border, is a favorite picnic oasis for people traveling between Zion National Park and the Grand Canyon. The 40-acre tract preserves an old Mormon fort that was built to guard Pipe Spring—the only source of water for many miles. You can browse through the fort, then retreat to the shady picnic grounds for lunch. In addition to the historic fort and two other buildings, you'll find many of the original tools and furnishings used by the pioneers. A member of the National Park Service is available daily, all day, to guide visitors through the buildings.

Side trips from old Route 66

Cutting across the northern highlands of Arizona, U.S. Highway 66 is one of the most-traveled east-west highways in the nation. This route provides access to the greatest concentration of scenic wonders in the Southwest. You pass from cactus desert to high, barren mesa lands, to irregular stands of juniper, and to splendid forests of Ponderosa pine. You may find yourself irritated by the billboards, auto junkyards, and curio shops along the way, but Route 66 does carry you through some spectacular country. If you venture off the highway, you will find such special places as Lake Mead and the lower Colorado River, the tiny Shangri-La of the Havasupai Indians, the Grand Canyon, and the Monument Valley empire of the Navajo.

You can also discover forests of petrified wood, a waterfall higher than Niagara, cinder cones, and several untapped miniature versions of the Grand Canyon.

Over most of its length, old Route 66 now has a combined designation: U.S. Highway 66 and Interstate Highway 40. The latter is a divided freeway. Interstate 40 departs from the path of U.S. 66 between Kingman and Ash Fork. U.S. 66 carries transcontinental traffic on a longer loop northward between the two towns.

The Grand Canyon and Monument Valley are covered in detail in other chapters of this book. Here are some notes on other side roads and scenic highlights of the 398-mile stretch of this highway between Topock, Arizona, and Gallup, New Mexico.

Many of the side roads mentioned in this chapter are unimproved; driving on them is subject to the cautions listed in the introductory chapter.

THE COLORADO RIVER

Attractions on the lower Colorado River include Lake Havasu to the south, narrow Lake Mohave and Black Canyon to the north, and Hoover Dam and vast Lake Mead farther north. Visitors can enjoy water sports, fishing, cruising on the Colorado River and cooling at its banks. Facilities include resorts, fishing camps, marinas, trailer parks, and public campgrounds. In some spots the river glides quietly through broad valleys, and in others it worms through narrow, cliff-walled canyons. Since there are no rapids here, traffic up and down the river is constant. (For the river south of Parker, see Southwestern Arizona, page 100.)

Topock Gorge

A scenic stretch of the Colorado River, accessible only by boat, lies just below Topock where Interstate Highway 40 crosses the river. Mohave Canyon, 15 miles in length, leads to 40-mile-long Lake Havasu, a narrow and intensely blue body of water that takes its name from the Indian word for blue water. Neither roads nor trails approach Mohave Canyon, but the vacationist with a boat can explore the bays, sloughs, caves,

BELOW HOOVER DAM, the Black Canyon of the Colorado stretches for 20 miles.

and side canyons that cut into the steep, colorful walls. Boats and motors can be rented at Shorty's Camp at Topock, and there is a free launching ramp there for those who bring their own boats.

Lake Havasu

Lake Havasu is a refreshing break in the stark desert, its blue water edged with green tamarisks or tule marsh. This Colorado River reservoir fluctuates so little it has been spared the shoreline band that disfigures most reservoirs.

Lake Havasu State Park, a 13,000-acre preserve, has its headquarters at Pittsburgh Point on the Lake Havasu City airport island. Check with the ranger for information on the many campsites around the lake. Lake Havasu has no shoreline road. Roads penetrate to the shoreline at only six points—for boat launching. Five of these points have resorts, boating facilities (including rental), and trailer parks; four of them have camping spaces.

The urban development of Lake Havasu City, the new site of England's London Bridge, is also located on Lake Havasu.

From any base on the shore, you can spend a full day just exploring by boat. This sinuous lake is only 3 miles across at its widest point, but it extends nearly 32 miles from its upper end just below Blankenship Bend to the tip of the Bill Williams Arm at Parker Dam.

A STARTLING SIGHT greets visitors to Lake Havasu City where the London Bridge connects the airport island with a London village.

Water-skiers can combine a lake-length voyage with some good skiing. You can ski for an hour in one direction uninterrupted, if you have the endurance; there's plenty of room for distance runs and great sweeping turns. Powerful winter winds can turn the lake into a choppy sea. These usually taper off by March, but if one occurs, plenty of sheltered-water refuges are strung along the shore. Havasu is narrow enough that it does not develop waves as big as those, for example, on Lake Mead.

Anglers like Havasu for many reasons; one of the best is the concurrence of the best fishing seasons with the pleasantest weather—in the spring and fall months. There is no closed season, and you may fish all day and all night.

To reach the lake, turn south off U.S. 66 on Arizona State Highway 95 about 10 miles east of Topock. It's about 20 miles to Lake Havasu City on its eastern shore.

Lake Havasu City. Here in the desert is a sun-drenched city carefully planned from the start for a balanced mix of residential and light industrial development. Started in 1963 on the east shore of the blue lake, it now has a population of over 12,000. Its most intriguing feature is the real London Bridge, dismantled over the Thames, shipped 10,000 miles, and rebuilt here. The city has several major motels and motor hotels, rental apartments, good restaurants and lounges, and all the services one would expect in a modern city.

Activities include the London Bridge Regatta in the spring, national boat and water-ski competitions, and the annual London Bridge Anniversary Celebration, a week-long event in early October. The marina, across the London Bridge on the airport island and adjacent to the Nautical Inn, has 410 slips, boat rentals, and fuel dock. Other facilities include a tackle store and rentals, ski equipment and rentals, boat and motor repairs, dry storage, and a big launching ramp.

The airport, one of Arizona's busiest, hosts scheduled airline jets and many private planes, including amphibians. Nearby are a trailer park (by reservation only) and a Crazy Horse campground by the lake. About 3½ miles north of the bridge, off State 95, is a KOA campground.

Ghost towns

The paved, two-lane road north of Topock through Oatman and Goldroad was U.S. 66 before that road was rerouted south through Sac-

THE FALL AND RISE OF THE LONDON BRIDGE

Everyone seems to have an opinion about the presence in Arizona of this historical British bridge. To some Arizonans, the bridge, its granite scoured clean of London grime and its bright flags snapping in the breeze, is more at home on the desert than on the Thames. Others feel that, while visually stunning, it is a massive anachronism. And visiting Londoners might view the whole phenomenon as an American threat to everything British—wondering, perhaps, if Buckingham Palace may be next to appear at Lake Havasu. The only way to make up your own mind as to whether London Bridge is at home on the American desert is to visit it yourself.

Although authentic, it's not the original London Bridge, nor is it the last. The first rude span across the Thames must have been built by Roman Legionnaires. A number of wooden London bridges followed, well-suited for burning. The first stone bridge was completed in 1205.

The bridge now in Arizona was the second stone bridge, opened in 1831. In 1902 it was widened by hanging the sidewalks over the sides. But by the late 1960s it was obviously no longer fit for modern traffic, for it was gradually sinking into the river bed. In 1968 the city of London put it up for sale.

Robert McCulloch, founder of Lake Havasu City, and C. V. Wood, Jr., its master planner, saw the opportunity to make it an important and unique attraction and offered 2½ million dollars. It took another $5.6 million to dismantle the 130,000 tons of granite, ship them 10,000 miles to Southern California, truck them across the desert, and reassemble them over a structural steel and concrete core. The project was the epitome of master planning: the bridge was built first on dry land, then the mile-long channel now separating the airport island from the shore was excavated beneath it.

The Lord Mayor of London laid the cornerstone in September, 1968, and a gala celebration marked the bridge's opening in October, 1971. An English village sits beside the bridge, complete with village pub, restaurant, and shops. A London doubledecker bus is parked on the waterfront.

---

ramento Wash. By taking this 54-mile detour, you add 9 miles to your trip but escape for awhile the heavy traffic of U.S. 66. The road is no longer well-maintained; you can expect numerous chuckholes and washboards.

Oatman. Reviving and very much alive as a winter tourist center, Oatman has an attraction for artists and their patrons and collectors of frontier relics. It's named for Olive Oatman, a pioneer girl who survived an Apache massacre near Gila Bend and years of captivity by the Mohave Indians (the Apaches traded her for horses) to return to normal frontier life. The town was founded in 1911 and thrived during the next two decades on mining operations in the surrounding Ute Mountains. During one 3½-year bonanza period, the United Eastern Mine produced more than $18 million in gold. The town once boasted dozens of businesses, seven hotels, 20 saloons, and a stock exchange; just prior to the Depression, Oatman's population exceeded 12,300. In 1941, after Congress suspended the mining of non-strategic materials, the mines closed.

Today, a revived hotel (18 rooms, lounge, and cafe), service station, grocery store, art gallery, and curio shops line Oatman's single paved street. Among the sagging frame structures up on the hills are some that have been reclaimed, along with small homes and mobiles.

Goldroad. Two miles east of Oatman and entirely deserted, the decaying buildings and eroded adobe walls that are the remains of Goldroad sprawl down the steep slopes west of Sitgreaves Pass.

Gold was discovered here in 1902, and the precipitous townsite was not abandoned until World War II. In 1953, all of the remaining buildings were razed or rendered unusable to release them from the tax rolls.

Today it looks like an ancient Pueblo Indian ruin, except for the weathered wood windowframes. Weeds and lizards flourish among the crumbling walls, and a rustling wind flaps rusting sheets of corrugated roofing. Though it's picked clean of relics and mining artifacts, it's very photogenic.

(Continued on next page)

RAFT ARRIVES at Colorado River arm of Lake Mead after 9-day trip through Grand Canyon. Lake Mead, the reservoir behind Hoover Dam, provides a 250-square-mile water playground.

If you do spend some time exploring the old townsites, use particular care while investigating tailing dumps, crumbling walls, and rickety buildings. The slopes surrounding both towns are honeycombed with abandoned mine shafts, often partially concealed by debris.

LAKE MEAD NATIONAL RECREATION AREA

At Kingman, U.S. 93 heads northwest to the Lake Mead National Recreation Area. From Hoover Dam north and east to the canyons of the Virgin and Colorado rivers, Lake Mead offers vast, rock-walled gorges and endless bays and inlets to be explored. The back country pro-vides an almost limitless field for auto-exploring on the maze of secondary roads winding through miles of rugged terrain. You'll see forests of Joshua trees and juniper, petroglyphs, ghost towns and abandoned mines, and water holes where desert wildlife comes to drink.

To the south of Hoover Dam, the Colorado River has sliced deep into a thousand feet of volcanic rock to produce the spectacular gorge called Black Canyon at the upper end of Lake Mohave, which also is in the Lake Mead National Recreation Area.

Almost a hundred miles of the length of the Grand Canyon lies in the eastern half of the Lake Mead National Recreation Area. It is unsurveyed country that's hard to get into, but it's full of exciting finds. You can approach it by turning off U.S. 93 on the Pierce Ferry road, 25½ miles northwest of Kingman.

A rich archeological dig on the Colorado was uncovered near Willow Beach, below the dam on what is now Lake Mohave. Most publicized of tourist attractions is a collection of relics from the "Lost City," Pueblo Grande de Nevada, a group of pueblo dwellings in the Moapa Valley near Overton, Nevada, that date from 1 A.D. Rising waters of Lake Mead covered most of the villages, but many of the artifacts that were carefully removed are on exhibit in the Lost City Museum, operated by the state of Nevada at Overton.

For brochures giving complete information on the whole area, write to Superintendent, Lake Mead National Recreational Area, 601 Nevada Highway, Boulder City, Nevada 98005, or stop there or at the visitor center at the turnoff to Boulder Beach from U.S. 93 just west of Hoover Dam.

Lake Mohave

Unlike spreading Lake Mead, Lake Mohave is confined for its whole length between hills or steep canyon walls. It spreads 4 miles at its widest point, but most of it is hardly more than a deeper, clearer, calmer Colorado River, with a few bays and estuaries. At an altitude of about 600 feet, with surrounding mountain ranges reaching to almost a mile above it, this pleasant stretch of water extends for 65 miles from Davis Dam to Hoover Dam.

While the area is ringed by the blacktops of U.S. Highways 95, 66, and 93, and Lake Mohave itself is accessible by road at several points, you can bridge the Colorado between Topock and Hoover Dam only at Davis Dam, reached from the east by Arizona Highway 68 and from the west by Nevada Highway 77. To circle the lake north of Davis Dam takes about 4 hours. But for the desert explorer, this perimeter swing should be only a preliminary reconnaissance. Away from the main travel routes, you'll find a clean, flinty-hard, sparkling kind of desert, sweeping up from the river to fantastic crests as high as 5,500 feet.

There is no closed season on any of the fish species. The purchase of a reciprocal stamp with the license of either Arizona or Nevada entitles you to fish on either side of the lake or the river. Licenses and stamps may be obtained at lakeshore concessions. You'll find boats and marina facilities, trailer parks, campgrounds, overnight accommodations, and restaurants at Willow Beach, reached on a 4-mile paved road

that turns off U.S. 93 about 14 miles south of Hoover Dam; Katherine, just north of Davis Dam; and Cottonwood Cove, 15 miles east of Searchlight in Nevada.

Hoover Dam

The setting of Hoover Dam, the massive concrete wedge between the sheer walls of Black Canyon, is unbelievably barren. In place of trees and shrubs, a forest of skeletal high-tension power towers leans over the brink of the canyon and strides away over the harsh hills. Only the blue water behind the dam, stretching out of sight between more of the flinty hills, and the blue sky relieve the lunarlike landscape.

The dam rises 726 feet from the streambed below, but there's no way to get below the dam to view its towering face from the bottom. However, there's an overlook on the road up out of the canyon on the west that gives you a view of its entire face from above.

The Bureau of Reclamation conducts continual tours of the dam throughout the day. Visitors descend by elevator into the interior of the dam to the enormous generating plant below; a guide explains the dam's hydroelectric function and tells the story of its construction. You can park behind the exhibit building at the west end of the dam. In the building you'll see an animated model of a generator and a topographical model of the entire Colorado River drainage basin. Snacks and soft drinks are available at a stand nearby.

Lake Mead

Roughly Y-shaped, Lake Mead points one of its arms north to the mouth of the Virgin River; the other twists east toward the Colorado. You can stay in a motel or camp on the shore, rent a small boat or launch your own. Since the water level of Lake Mead fluctuates from year to year, the National Park Service and its concessionaires have provided facilities for recreational activities that can be moved up and down the beaches as the water rises or recedes. The National Park Service provides free paved launching ramps at all of the developed marina areas.

When you are boating on the lake, shoals and underwater rocks require close watch and slow speed near the shore or in shallow areas. For safety on fast distance runs, stick to the river channel marked on charts and topographic maps. Lake Mead charts are for sale at most marinas and ranger stations; topographic maps and lake charts are for sale at Lake Mead Visitor Center.

There are launching and docking facilities, boat rentals, and fishermen's supplies (including licenses and bait) at Lake Mead Marina, Las Vegas Boat Harbor, Callville Bay, Echo Bay, and Overton Beach in Nevada; and at Temple Bar in Arizona. Only launching ramps and courtesy dock are available at Hemenway Harbor. Lake Mead Marina also offers cruises. Charter boats are available at all of these areas. You can arrange to be taken to a camping spot, to be brought supplies, and to be picked up at a pre-arranged time.

Make reservations for berthing your boat anywhere considerably in advance. The boating population is growing faster than the facilities.

Improved campgrounds are maintained by the National Park Service at Boulder Beach, Temple Bar, Echo Bay, Callville Bay, and Las Vegas Bay. Boulder Beach is excellent for swimming; lifeguards are on duty during the summer season.

All of the above-listed campgrounds include space for trailers. In addition, there are concession trailer courts at Boulder Beach, Temple Bar, Echo Bay, and Overton Beach.

For the boat camper there are good coves near Boulder Canyon, on Overton Arm and the Boulder Islands, and at Greggs Basin, Sandy Point, and Driftwood Cove.

If you're not a camper, you'll find accommodations at Lake Mead Lodge near Boulder Beach (motel rooms, swimming pool), Temple Bar Resort (motel and cafe), Echo Bay (hotel and restaurants), and Overton Beach Motel. Motels are available in nearby Boulder City and in Las Vegas, Overton, and Kingman. Motel reservations are essential during spring and fall peak fishing seasons, particularly for Easter and Memorial Day holidays.

The National Park Service offers illustrated naturalist programs at Boulder Beach camp.

Temple Bar

A paved, 2-lane road east off U.S. 93 about 18 miles south of Hoover Dam takes you to the resort of Temple Bar. The road travels the wide valley of Detrital Wash and approaches the often incredibly blue southern arm of the lake over low, rolling hills peppered with fragments of porous black lava. As you enter the settlement, the contrast with the harsh desert is immediate and refreshing. The National Park Service campground is shaded by tall palms and eucalyptus, brightened by red and white flowers of glossy oleanders. The concessionaire's trailer village is in a grove of cottonwoods.

KINGMAN TO FLAGSTAFF

Kingman, the seat of Mohave County, is the principal stopover point along this section of U.S. Highway 66. It has become a travel center because of its location at the junction of U.S. 66 (Interstate 40) and U.S. 93. The Kingman Area Chamber of Commerce Tourist Center and Museum, located at the junction of the two highways, is open weekdays. The center provides information about points of interest in Mohave County and will help the visitor plan interesting side trips in the area. The museum, devoted to Mohave County historical material, is open weekdays and afternoons on Saturday and Sunday.

Hualapai Mountain Park

The upland forest of Hualapai Mountain Park near Kingman surrounds one of the highest peaks in western Arizona. It offers a respite from highway driving and a cool place for a picnic or for camping.

To reach the park, take U.S. 66-93 east from Kingman. The road to the park starts a mile and a half east of the junction of U.S. 93 and 66. In the half-hour drive (14 miles), you go from desert to mountain pines.

Set among the trees in the park are picnic tables, grills, campsites, and water faucets. There are cabins for rent (furnished with beds, refrigerators, and hot plates; bring your own bedding and cooking utensils).

A mile beyond the park, Hualapai Lodge offers meals and overnight accommodations.

The Hualapai Indian Reservation

Peach Springs, in the juniper hills 50 miles east of Kingman on U.S. 66, is the headquarters and trading center of the Hualapai Indian Reservation, which covers almost a million acres along about 110 miles of the Colorado River's south bank. The tribe numbers about 1400, of which about half live on the reservation. The Indians invite hunters but require tribal permits and compliance with state game laws.

For a small fee you can visit the reservation, and an additional small fee allows you to camp anywhere on it, but there are no improved campsites. You'll find water year-round at Frazier's Wells, 25 miles northeast of Peach Springs on a graded road 8,000 feet high in a pine forest. Elsewhere, carry your own and be prepared for unimproved and unmapped roads.

About 25 miles north of Peach Springs on another gravel road is Diamond Creek and the first access to the Colorado River below Phantom Ranch. River runners touch shore here to pick up supplies. The scenic road is adequate for light cars and pickups, except after a heavy rain.

For information on visiting the reservation and for hunting arrangements, write to Hualapai Wildlife and Outdoor Recreation, P.O. Box 216, Peach Springs, AZ 86434.

Havasupai Indian Reservation

Clear, turquoise-blue Havasu Creek gushes out of the ground to water the tiny, remote Havasupai Indian Reservation, a 518-acre, idyllic canyon oasis and the home of 300 of the tribe.

You can visit their village, explore the narrow canyon and the long waterfalls below it, stay overnight in the Indians' motel-like lodges, and do your own cooking. Or you can camp out in a nearby Indian campground. But to get there, you'll either have to hike or ride a horse 8 miles from the roadhead, which is 62 miles by seasonal dirt roads from the nearest point on U.S. 66, or arrange an expensive helicopter flight.

How to get there. To drive to the parking place above the canyon, you start about 7 miles east of Peach Springs on U.S. 66. Turn off north on the dirt road to Frazier's Wells and Hualapai Hilltop. Paved for about 40 miles, it turns unpaved for the next 22 miles. Ask first about road conditions at Peach Springs.

There's ample parking space at Hualapai Hilltop. If you have made advance arrangements, you arrive in time to meet the pack train the Indians have brought up from the village (one horse for you, one for your luggage). Riders can carry camera and canteen, but that's all.

It's a hot, dusty 6 miles, dropping 2,000 feet to the creek—a good picnic spot—and 2 more miles to the village. Summer heat may top 110°

The village and falls. The trail widens to become the main street of the village. At its center are two guest lodges, snack bar, a post office (the last one served by pack train), and a tourist office at which visitors register and pay a small trail fee. Small homes, including a few pre-fabs flown in by helicopter, are scattered among the cottonwoods, willows, and occasional small orchards.

Major attractions are the three beautiful waterfalls in the canyon below the village. Mooney Falls, the farthest, 3 miles downstream, is 196 feet high, higher than Niagara Falls. You can clamber down a cliff and swim in a pool below, wondering at the rock-frosting of minerals deposited by the blue-green water. You can rent a horse in the village to ride to Havasu Falls, and hike the last mile to Mooney Falls where the trail dwindles and almost disappears down the Colorado River.

Staying overnight. The Indians can put you up in one of their lodges or private rooms for a small charge per person per night. You cook in a community kitchen, utensils and dishes provided, and you can buy groceries at the store, or eat at the village snack bar. Or you can camp at the Indian campground 2½ miles below the village, with water, picnic tables, grates, and pit toilets. The tribe has another campground at Navajo Falls, 1½ miles below the village. Bring your own fuel or buy white gas or Sterno at the store. A fee is charged for camping, and reservations are required.

Reservations. Make reservations for saddle and pack horses and for accommodations by writing to the Havasupai Tourist Enterprise, Supai, AZ 86435, or telephone (602) 448-2121. Campers can reserve sites by telephoning or by writing to "Campground Reservations" at the same address. Reserve or confirm reservations by the telephone at Hualapai Hilltop before heading down the trail.

Grand Canyon Caverns

Fourteen miles east of Peach Springs, Grand Canyon Caverns offers a cool stopping place if you are driving U.S. 66 in summer.

On the tour you'll see caves in an early stage of stalactite-stalagmite formation. The water that formed them drained away long ago as the Colorado River cut below their level deeper into nearby Grand Canyon.

The caverns are open daily to visitors, and tours are conducted throughout the day. There's a small fee.

Williams

Located at the road junction offering the shortest route from Interstate 40 to Grand Canyon Village, Williams is a popular stopover for tourists headed for the canyon. This friendly town caters to the traveler's needs, and offers a choice of dining and lodging accommodations. There are Forest Service campgrounds a few miles from town at Cataract and Kaibab lakes.

Some of the best views of the countryside are seen from the summit of Bill Williams Mountain, 4 miles south of Williams.

The moderate winters bring enough snow to turn the mountain into a winter sports area suitable for both beginning and intermediate skiers. A 1,500-foot Poma lift (450-foot vertical rise) and a 700-foot rope tow are operated on weekends and holidays. A lodge, ski rentals, and a snack bar are available to skiers.

Eighteen miles southeast of Williams, White Horse Lake is tucked away in the Ponderosa pine country of Kaibab National Forest. Each spring the Arizona Game and Fish Department stocks the lake with several thousand legal-sized rainbow trout. The Forest Service maintains campsites with tables, fireplaces, and some trailer spaces (limit 14 days). A lakeside concessionaire has housekeeping cabins, a small store selling groceries and fishing tackle, and rowboats and paddleboats for rent. No motorboats are permitted on the lake.

To reach White Horse Lake from Williams, follow the paved Perkinsville road (Fourth St.) south for 8 miles to a marked intersection; turn left, and continue another 10 miles to the lake.

Sycamore Canyon

A rugged gorge 17 miles long and as deep as 2,000 feet, Sycamore Canyon roughly parallels Oak Creek Canyon, which it resembles topographically. But the resemblance ends there, for it's the core of a 46,000-acre primitive area reserved for hikers and horseback riders. Its northernmost tip stretches to within a mile or two of White Horse Lake, and you can reach an overlook on the rim by following a very rough dirt road, normally passable in a passenger car in dry weather, from the White Horse Lake road from Williams. The marked turnoff is 16 miles from town and 2 miles short of the lake. From the rim you see a maze of eroded red sandstone, white limestone and dark brown lava, and the sycamore-shaded creek channel.

In some years an autumn trail ride is guided

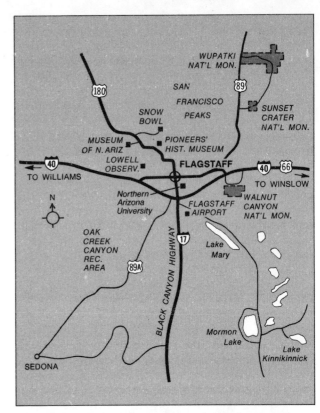

FLAGSTAFF area features variety of attractions, interesting loop trips, snowy winter weather.

into the canyon from Perkinsville, between Prescott and Williams. For information on pack trips and hiking trails, ask at the ranger stations at Williams or Sedona or write to the Supervisors of Coconino National Forest, 114 North San Francisco Street, Flagstaff, AZ 86001; the Kaibab National Forest, 800 S. 6th Street, Williams, AZ 86046; or the Prescott National Forest, 344 South Cortex, Prescott, AZ 86301. All three national forests border the area.

THE FLAGSTAFF AREA

Unofficial capital of northern Arizona, Flagstaff is the hub of a fascinating area. Many tourists stop here to enjoy the city's close-in attractions or to use it as a base for exploring the surrounding country in one or two-day loop trips.

Because of its 6,900-foot altitude, Flagstaff may have snow anytime from October through May and surely during January, February, and March. Average annual snowfall is 73 inches, but because of the low humidity, the snow cover rapidly melts, and snow removal after a storm is prompt. However, if you drive to Flagstaff during the winter, check first with the highway patrol on road conditions. You may need chains during and immediately after a storm.

Summers are moderate (for Arizona) at this altitude. Temperatures in June, the warmest month, may reach the low 90s. During July and August, afternoon showers cool the pine forests and the more-than-mile-high city.

If you are going to explore Flagstaff and its environs, make a first stop at the Chamber of Commerce (at U.S. 66 and Beaver Street) for maps, guide books, and specific directions for 10 different drive-yourself tours found on the back of the city street map. These include tours to Sunset Crater and Wupatki Ruins, the South Rim of the Grand Canyon, Walnut Canyon, and to Sedona and Oak Creek Canyon.

Events

Each Fourth of July the city produces a colorful celebration known as the All-Indian Pow-Wow. This three-day festival attracts thousands of brightly costumed Indians who come to participate in or simply to watch the daytime parades and rodeos and evening ceremonial dances. A spectacular show, the Pow-Wow attracts tourists in large numbers.

The Summer Festival is a two week or longer series of cultural activities. The Flagstaff Symphony Orchestra presents concerts and guest soloists, as well as guest musicians augmenting its regular sections. The Northern Arizona University drama department and guest actors present plays; other attractions include children's performances, film classics, and art exhibits.

Lowell Observatory

Observatory domes aren't framed in wood these days, but they were when Lowell Observatory was built back in 1894. Nearly hidden in a pine forest on a 7,250-foot hilltop at the outskirts of Flagstaff, the observatory appears rather unimposing as you view it from a distance. But its domed buildings house seven separate telescopes and an impressive collection of data on our solar system.

The observatory staff offers a lecture followed by a guided tour at 1:30 p.m. Monday through Friday. In addition to viewing the 24″ refractor telescope, you're welcome to visit the library in the main administration building and to study the large collection of telescopic photographs on display there.

From June through August, weather permitting, the observatory offers free slide lectures and star gazing on Friday evenings. Get tickets in advance from the Flagstaff Chamber of Commerce.

Flagstaff's "moon lab"

On Cedar Avenue atop McMillan Mesa is the headquarters building of the U.S. Geological Survey's Center of Astrogeology. Although no tours are offered, interested visitors will see exhibits in the reception area describing the geologic mapping of the moon, research in formation of craters, and training of the astronauts in lunar geology. Studies here supported the space exploration program of the National Aeronautics and Space Administration. Nearby Sunset Crater and Meteor Crater (see pages 33 and 37) served as field laboratories for the testing of lunar exploration methods and equipment and the training of the United States astronauts.

ZUNI WOMEN, serenely balancing pots on their heads, parade in Flagstaff's All-Indian Pow-Wow.

A scenic route to Grand Canyon

U.S. 180 between Flagstaff and the South Rim of the Grand Canyon is a scenic, 79-mile drive pleasant at any time of year. In spring the highway is lined with the bright reds, blues, and yellows of high-country wildflowers. During summer the dark green of pines and junipers stands out vividly against the red volcanic earth, and billowing thunderheads pile high in the afternoon sky. Autumn brings the golden hues of aspen to the roadside; and often, before the brilliant leaves have fallen to the ground, heavy snows sweep down from lofty San Francisco Peaks to cloak the land in white. Snowplows keep the road open to traffic.

Pioneers' Historical Museum. Located 2 miles from downtown Flagstaff on U.S. 180, this museum is housed in an old tufa rock building that is historically interesting for itself (it was originally a county hospital), as well as for the relics it contains of early northern Arizona pioneers —antique pictures, furniture, personal belongings. Behind the main building is a barn full of vintage tools, stoves, and fire equipment.

To the rear of that barn is the "Art Barn" (Flagstaff Arts and Crafts Center), focal point of a vigorous local artistic movement.

The museum is open daily and Sunday afternoons from mid-April to mid-October. Admission is free.

Museum of Northern Arizona. Flagstaff's Museum of Northern Arizona is one of the most authoritative sources on the geology, biology and anthropology of Arizona and on Indian arts and crafts. Surrounded by a pine forest with the creek channel behind it, the handsome, tile-roofed stone buildings sit back off U.S. 180 behind an arch of timber on pillars of native stone. It's a mile north of the Pioneers' Historical Museum, on the opposite side of the road.

Three of the six exhibit rooms deal with the natural history of northern Arizona. Dioramas, relief maps, pictures, and charts graphically explain the formation and subsequent history of prominent physical features such as Sunset Crater, San Francisco Peaks, Oak Creek Canyon, and Meteor Crater. Plant and animal exhibits (including a summer display of native wildflowers) illustrate individual species in various habitats, ranging from desert to arctic-alpine life zones. One display shows the effect of rainfall and altitude on plant life.

The remaining three rooms contain extensive exhibits of Indian arts and crafts (mainly

AUTUMN on San Francisco Peaks precedes winter snows that transform summits to a skiers' world.

Hopi and Navajo). Visitors can buy authentic Indian craft products from a museum shop at the rear; here you will find one of the best collections in the state. The museum has done much to encourage Indian artisans and develop public appreciation of their work.

The annual Hopi Craftsman Show is held in July at the museum. In addition to displays of craftwork, demonstrations are given in weaving, pottery, and basket-making techniques. One of the show's most popular traditions is Hopi piki bread; you can buy a roll of this thinly layered blue cornmeal treat, hot from a stone griddle.

Offering year around enjoyment, the museum is open daily and on Sunday afternoons. Admission is free.

Arizona Snow Bowl. Located on the northwest slopes of San Francisco Peaks, this famed resort is the oldest and best-known ski resort in Arizona. The 6,800-foot double chairlift takes you to 11,600 feet near the top of Mt. Agassiz, a vertical rise of 2,100 feet. Four handle tows, a Poma lift, and a rope tow also serve skiers. A ski rental shop, lounge, and snack bar are open during the season, which usually runs from late November to late March.

Summer visitors also can ride the chairlift; the top, well above timberline, affords a sweeping view. You can take an easy walk up the mountain to several small, wildflower-strewn meadows or try a more strenuous climb—past stunted bristlecone pines and over lava cinders and rock slabs—up the remaining 500 feet or so to the Agassiz summit.

Ambitious hikers can make a day of it by going 4 miles to the top of nearby Humphreys Peak, highest point in Arizona (12,670 feet).

For information, write to Arizona Snow Bowl, Box 158, Flagstaff, AZ 86002, or telephone (602) 774-0562.

A swing off U.S. 89

Two diverse but fascinating national monuments are reached by a scenic loop off U.S. 89, itself a scenic drive north from the northeast corner of Flagstaff. In the first few miles you have the San Francisco Peaks to your left above green meadows framed by dark pine forests. The turnoff eastward to Sunset Crater is about 15 miles north of Flagstaff.

Sunset Crater. The great cinder cone of the extinct volcano, named for the red and yellow hues of the rim, dominates the landscape. During 4 to 6 months of eruption in the winter of 1064-65 (according to tree-ring studies), it threw out a billion tons of lava and ash over 800 square miles, destroying the pit houses of the Indians who lived in the area. But the volcanic ash, mulching and enriching the soil, created fertile land that drew Indians of four different cultures to the new kind of farming.

At the visitor center, 2 miles east of U.S. 89, are graphic exhibits of the history of the entire volcanic field, specimens of volcanic bombs, and seismographs continually recording the world's tremors. Across the road is a 45-unit Forest Service improved campground.

Wupatki National Monument. About 18 miles north on the same paved road is Wupatki National Monument, enclosing more than 800 ruins of villages of the Indians who moved in to take advantage of the fertile fields. The largest structure—Wupatki (Hopi for "tall house") —during the twelfth century was more than 3 stories high and contained more than 100 rooms. The visitor center displays the historical artifacts of the Indians who met and mingled here; they exchanged agricultural techniques, tools, arts, and crafts. Nearby is the smaller Lomaki ruin, and 9 miles north is the Citadel, another large structure still unexcavated.

Oak Creek Canyon and Sedona

Less than an hour south of Flagstaff on U.S. 89A is one of the best-known landmarks in Arizona, the famed and much-photographed Oak Creek Canyon and, in its lower end, the picture-postcard town of Sedona.

Although U.S. 89A enters the top of the canyon just a few miles south of Flagstaff, switching down the steep, forested canyon wall below a series of fine overlook points, the recommended approach is from the south. It is from the lower end that you get the full impact of the huge red rock formations that have made this area in Arizona second only to the Grand Canyon as a scenic attraction.

The Canyon. For the most dramatic approach to the canyon, follow State 179, which turns north toward Sedona from Interstate 17 about 45 miles south of Flagstaff. In sweeping curves you drive through sagebrush country brightened with sycamore-lined washes, and the earth itself begins to change color, from white to orange to red. Within 6 or 7 miles, you glimpse the erosion-carved buttes ahead, then a curve brings the first full view of brilliant temples and cliffs, always startling when first seen at full scale in this spacious setting.

The famous multi-spired Cathedral Rock (reproduced on wall calendars all over the world), Bell Rock, and several other eroded

RUINS of Sinagua Indian dwellings are preserved in Wupatki National Monument.

giants are in the open end of the canyon south of Sedona. Others surround the town itself, forming a vivid backdrop from any angle.

North of the town the canyon rises, narrows, and gradually changes character, becoming cool and densely wooded. The vertical rock walls give away to steep slopes of dark pine forest, though here and there a bare cliff face appears. In this upper canyon are 9 improved Forest Service campgrounds, almost always fully occupied except in winter, and many commercial resorts, lodges, trailer parks, and cabins. It's a favorite summer cooling-off place, offering many swimming holes along the creek and trout for anglers.

Numerous drives and hiking trails wind through this area, particularly in the lower end of the canyon. Schnebley Hill Road is a popular drive which climbs eastward from Sedona and winds up to Interstate 17, yielding excellent views of the big rocks to the southwest.

Sedona. Sedona reflects community effort to incorporate and combine the best of frontier styles and contemporary materials, rejecting contemporary neon and plastic disfigurations. In this setting of eroded redrock mesas and pillars towering behind every store-front and residence, the town does not insult nature.

The town's businesses include art galleries, crafts shops, Indian arts and crafts stores, and antique shops, a number of motels, rental cabins, and trailer parks in or around the town. Several large motels at its south end afford excellent views across Oak Creek. For information on accommodations and recreation activities, write to the Sedona-Oak Creek Chamber of Commerce, P.O. Box 478, Sedona, AZ 86336.

The forest lakes

To the south of Flagstaff is a chain of forest-rimmed lakes offering a variety of fishing and water recreation opportunities. All are reached by the same Lake Mary Road turning southeast off U.S. 89A about 3 miles south of Flagstaff.

All the lakes are at around 7,000 feet in elevation. The best fishing usually runs from May through September.

The Verde Valley

In the back country of north-central Yavapai County, the Verde River rises and winds east and south for almost 130 miles to join the Salt River near Phoenix. Before it reaches that junction, the Verde flows through remote rocky channels that are wildly beautiful and almost inaccessible.

But in the middle reaches of its course, it crosses a broad basin of rolling range, roughly 25 by 40 miles, bounded by the metallic Black Hills on the southwest and west, the tinted walls of the Mogollon Rim on the north and east, and Hackberry Mountain and the Mazatzals on the southeast. This irregular basin, southeast of Sedona, is the region known as the Verde Valley.

The cycles of time have left a graphic record here: pueblos of prehistoric Indians, frontier cavalry barracks, abandoned sites of modern mining industry, and an interesting former ghost town, now lively again.

EROSION-CARVED giants brighten Oak Creek Canyon, which climbs from desert to highlands.

Two approaches from Interstate 40 form western and eastern boundaries of this most attractive area: U.S. 89 south from Ash Fork and Interstate 17 south from Flagstaff. The most scenic route of all, U.S. 89A, originates in Flagstaff and goes diagonally southwestward to meet U.S. 89 north of Prescott. This is the route through Sedona in dramatic Oak Creek Canyon, taking you into the bottom of the valley, to the river crossing at Cottonwood, and up the slope of Mingus Mountain through the refurbished relics and new bustle of historic hillside Jerome. The road net creates many loop-trip possibilities from Flagstaff, Williams, and Prescott.

You'll find modern accommodations in the main communities (principally at Cottonwood, and Camp Verde) and at outlying resorts. Information is available from the Verde Valley Chamber of Commerce, Box 412, Cottonwood, and from the Sedona-Oak Creek Canyon Chamber of Commerce.

Cornville, Cottonwood, and Clarkdale. Side-road explorers will find several worthwhile destinations in the Cornville area: the sleepy hamlet itself on the banks of Oak Creek, the Page Springs Fish Hatchery, the Christian Indian School, and some Indian ruins in the vicinity of Sugarloaf Mesa.

The farming and cattle town of Cottonwood, an oasis on the Verde River shaded by groves of its namesake trees and the valley's principal trading center, is growing rapidly.

Clarkdale, whose huge smelter once processed copper ore from the rich Jerome mines, is now a quiet residential town. Just outside Clarkdale is Peck's Lake, a popular spot for water sports, adjacent to Verde Valley Country Club golf course.

Tuzigoot National Monument. Tuzigoot (Apache for "crooked water") is a major prehistoric Indian ruin on a ridge 2 miles east of Clarkdale. Built during the 12th century, it housed Indians who moved here when a severe drought dried up farmlands away from water resources. Abandoned in the early 15th century, the 110-room pueblo fell into ruin and was almost obscured until the 1930s, when it was completely excavated by University of Arizona archeologists.

Exhibits in the museum include a variety of grave offerings—turquoise mosaics, beads, bracelets of shells obtained by barter with Indians near the Gulf of California, and decorated pottery. Tuzigoot is open daily, and rangers will answer your questions.

Jerome. The former copper-mining center of Jerome, called by its boosters "America's Largest Ghost City," sits west of Clarkdale, high on the slope of Cleopatra Mountain, one of the Black Hills Range bounding the Verde Valley on the west.

From its peak in the 1920s, with a population of 15,000, the boom town dwindled to a ghost town as the ore deposits were exhausted. When the last mines closed in 1953, some of the town's 200 die-hards formed the Jerome Historical Society and began to call attention to its history, its quaint appearance, and its tourist value. Today the population is back to nearly 400, and tourists number over a million yearly.

The steep slope is covered with a casual mixture of sagging ghost-town hulks and rebuilt or newly-built residences, side-by-side on the serpentine streets; those on the downhill side are supported by stilts. There's an incomparable view across the Verde Valley to the cliffs of the Mogollon Rim and the red rock of Oak Creek Canyon. Artists, of course, love the area, and many have settled there. There's an art gallery and a number of antique and crafts stores. The Jerome State Historic Park Museum, occupying a former mine-owner's mansion, displays mining machinery and a fascinating three-dimensional see-through model of the maze of mine shafts riddling the ground beneath.

You can visit Jerome as part of a tour through Sedona and Oak Creek Canyon and other towns of the Verde Valley.

Camp Verde. Just 2 miles east of Interstate 17, about 41 miles south of Flagstaff, is the town of Camp Verde, and near the center of town is the Fort Verde State Historic Park. The park commemorates the garrison that served as a base of operations against the Apaches until 1885. Four of the original 20 buildings remain, and others are being restored as funds are obtained.

The visitor center displays the history and relics of the post. The Commanding Officer's house contains restored parlors, dining room, kitchen, and bedrooms. Two of the five one-room apartments in the Bachelor Officers' Quarters have been restored, and restoration of the post doctor's house is under way.

The old fort is open to visitors daily except on Christmas Day for a small admission fee. A picnic spot is nearby.

Montezuma Castle and Montezuma Well. Part of the dramatic impact of this famous apartment house cliff dwelling is due to its sudden appearance, high on the cliff, as you walk along a path from the national monument's handsome visitor center. The advantage held by the ancient Sinagua defenders is obvious. Visitors are no longer permitted to enter the well-preserved structure, but signs and exhibits, including a cut-away model, explain the prehistoric settlement. The walk marked Sycamore Trail takes only a few minutes; a keyed pamphlet available at the site tells what you are seeing.

Plan to spend some time in the visitor center, where you'll find excellent archeological and natural history displays.

Within a detached area of the Montezuma Castle National Monument, 7 miles northeast of the castle, is another surprise—a limestone sink creating a small lake (470 feet across, 55 feet deep), fringed with large trees within a crater-like depression in a low hill.

The calm, mysterious surface of Montezuma Well gives no hint that it is contributing 1½ million gallons of water a day to adjacent Beaver Creek and the area's irrigated farms.

The Indians who lived here centuries ago engineered an irrigation system to divert the water to their fields, and you can still see sections of the ditches. Ruins of their houses are visible along the trail. Be alert for rattlesnakes.

Drive back to Interstate 17 and turn southward on the highway for about 2½ miles to reach a roadside rest area marked by an observation tower. Picnic ramadas and restrooms make this a good picnic stop, and the top of the tower commands a memorable panorama of the Verde country.

FLAGSTAFF TO NEW MEXICO BORDER

Heading east from Flagstaff on Interstate 40, you pass through several miles of forested land; then the route strikes out across a high mesa: grasswood intermittently mantled with greasewood, sage, juniper, and piñon. The road passes rainbow-striped crags and mesas, crosses gorges cut through the plateau by the seasonal rivers, and runs over rolling range country. En route are the tremendous Meteor Crater, Petrified Forest and its long vistas of the Painted Desert, and turnoffs to the Mogollon Rim, the White Mountains, and the Navajo and Hopi Indian reservations.

In Winslow and Holbrook are good motel accommodations. Those who wish to get in some camping can head south into Apache-Sitgreaves National Forest. The headquarters is in Springerville.

The Winslow and Holbrook chambers of commerce are good sources of information.

Walnut Canyon National Monument

Walnut Canyon National Monument preserves the remains of more than 300 small Sinagua Indian cliff dwellings dating from the 12th century. To reach the monument from Flagstaff, drive east about 7 miles on Interstate 40 to the entrance road. The monument encompasses the 400-foot-deep, horseshoe-shaped canyon of now-dry Walnut Creek and includes a ¾-mile hiking trail that leads past ruins on the sides of a steep, rocky peninsula.

The Sinaguas first occupied the canyon about 1000 A.D. They applied masonry skills learned from other Pueblo Indian groups to wall up weathered limestone shelves in the canyon sides, creating a series of joined rooms. Overhanging rock protected the homes from weather, as well as from enemy attack.

From the monument's visitor center at the rim of the canyon, the marked trail drops a steep 185 feet to level out at the neck of the peninsula. From here it's an easy loop walk past about 25 cliffside rooms; the round trip will take you about 40 minutes. From the narrow trail you can see about a hundred more rooms notched in the cliffs across the canyon.

Walnut Canyon is open daily; you pay a small fee for admission. Picnic tables are situated near the visitor center.

The Grand Falls

When the spring runoff from the Mogollon Plateau snowpack keeps streams flowing full, a detour off Interstate 40 will lead you to one of the most surprising sights in all of the high desert: the roaring, plunging, 185-foot Grand Falls of the Little Colorado River.

The falls are seasonal, and sometimes in dry years they never do reach impressive size. Normally, though, they run during winter and the spring thaw, dry up in May, then flow again during the summer rains in July and August. It's advisable to inquire at Flagstaff or Winslow about the current level of the Little Colorado before deciding on the side trip.

To reach the falls, you can turn off Interstate 40 at either of two points: Winona, 17 miles east of Flagstaff, or the Leupp junction, 10 miles west of Winslow. For either route, inquire at the turnoff for exact directions. The Winona route is the shortest from the highway, about 20 miles; the last 8 miles are unpaved.

Meteor Crater

Almost a mile across, 3 miles around the top, and 570 feet deep, Meteor Crater, one of the West's most unusual natural wonders, has excited the interest of scientists and travelers from all over the world. To reach the crater, drive east from Flagstaff on Interstate 40 about 37 miles, where a paved road heads south 5 miles to the crater site.

Scientists generally agree that the crater was formed by the impact of a 60,000-ton meteoric mass of iron and nickel about 50,000 years ago. It disintegrated on impact and splashed nearly half a billion tons of rock over the surrounding surface. The rim of the crater rises 150 feet or more above the plain and is visible for miles as a white scar against the desert. U.S. astronauts came here to study crater geology and to rehearse their "moonwalk" sampling procedures.

Energetic visitors can take the steep, rocky trail down into the crater, where old mining equipment can be examined. When the weather is hot, it is best to forego this hike—there is no breeze at the bottom of the crater, and it catches the full impact of the sun.

A longer hike, but much easier, is the trail leading around the rim. It affords many excellent views, passing an abandoned camp where glass sand was once mined from underlying sandstone.

The modern air-conditioned museum on the north rim has excellent exhibits explaining the event; large fragments on display attract much interest. A recorded narration heard in the museum and at adjacent overlooks answers many questions. There's a small fee for admission.

The crater and museum, a snack bar, and gift shop with good Indian jewelry are open daily.

Navajo and Hopi land

The Navajo and Hopi Indian reservations described on pages 38-49 are only a few miles north as you drive Interstate 40 between Winslow and Gallup, and Navajo lands flank the highway on both sides as you approach the New Mexico border. You can enter this country by roads leading north from or near Winona, Leupp Corners, Winslow, Holbrook, Chambers, Houck, and Lupton. Most of these roads are unimproved; however, if you take State 87 or 77, you will be able to explore a good portion of the reservation without ever leaving the pavement.

Petrified Forest National Park

In Petrified Forest National Park you can view what is probably the world's largest, most colorful collection of petrified wood, logs, and cross-sections of ancient mineralized trees with infusions of agate, jasper, and other semi-precious stones. Found also in the park are ruins of Indian villages, petroglyphs, and overlooks of the Painted Desert.

The park is arranged in two blocks at the north and south ends of a corridor connected by 27 miles of paved road. There's a visitor center, restaurant, and gas station at each end.

The northern entrance is off Interstate 40 about 25 miles northeast of Holbrook. From here, north of the highway, a winding road follows the rim of the Painted Desert, giving both a close-up examination of the multi-colored layers of sand and distant views toward the northwest. It's a good place for a picnic and for sunset-watching. For walkers, conditions on the Painted Desert are excellent for cross-country hikes, especially in the fall. Rangers at the visitor centers can provide suggestions and issue permits for overnight hikes.

About 11 miles from the north entrance, in the narrow corridor to the south, are the Puerco Indian Ruins, low stone walls outlining a prehistoric Indian pueblo village, and Newspaper Rock, covered with scratched petroglyphs—a message center of the ancients.

Further south are the Tepees, small conical peaks shaped by erosion, and the Blue Mesa, where erosion has left petrified logs on pinnacles of sandstone.

Another 2 miles brings you to the Agate Bridge, a log more than 100 feet long with a 40-foot wash eroded beneath it, then to the Jasper Forest overlook of masses of mineralized logs littering the valley.

The main petrified wood exhibits are near the southern visitor center in the Rainbow Forest area. Here are the Giant Logs and cross-sections, along with a museum whose displays explain how the fallen trees became preserved as stone. There's a picnic area here. Access to U.S. 180 is about 18 miles southeast of Holbrook.

At either end you can pick up an explanatory guidebook with a map, and rangers are in attendance. The park is open during daylight hours all year. There's the usual small admission fee but no additional charge to see the museums and exhibits. Visitors are asked to help preserve the park for future generations by not disturbing any natural features (especially petrified wood).

Navajo-Hopi country

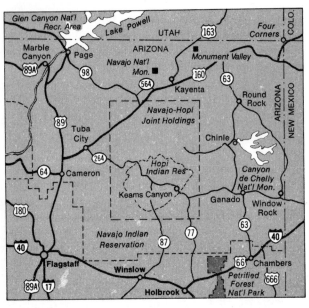

The dot in the distance grows larger. Finally you see it is an old man, standing beside the road. When you pull up and open the car door, he gets in without hesitation or comment, sits solemnly and silently for perhaps 5 miles, perhaps 20, then signals you to stop. At the roadside he nods his thanks, and heads off down the arid slope. There is no more evidence of human habitation here than at the point where you picked him up. You watch for a moment, then drive on. Obviously he knows where he is and where he is going.

Sometimes you need such a reminder as this old Navajo, when you are driving the vast expanse of his reservation, to reaffirm that the land is populated (actually over-populated in terms of its ability to support a pastoral economy). Despite the fact that a tribe that numbered 15,000 a century ago now totals more than 130,000 and despite new highways that have brought a surge of tourists, you gaze much of the time over seemingly unoccupied land.

There are at least three good reasons to visit the Navajo-Hopi country: to absorb its dramatic, sculptured-sandstone scenery; to inspect its archeological relics, evidence of an advanced civilization of a thousand years ago;

and to learn something about its present occupants, whose distinctive cultures have survived long after those of most North American tribes have all but disappeared.

Travelers with such interests have been wandering through this country for decades, but until recently they were a small fraternity. A principal requirement was a willingness to accept the mild discomforts and possible hazards of traveling long distances, far from any town, on primitive roads. Now pavement has penetrated much of the reservation and opened this remote and beautiful land to a new group of travelers as appreciative (if not as adventurous) as the pre-pavement pioneers.

The Navajo Indian Reservation, the nation's largest (more than 25,000 square miles), spills across state boundaries in northeastern Arizona, southeastern Utah, and northwestern New Mexico. The Hopi Indian Reservation and the surrounding Hopi-Navajo joint holdings (a portion of the old Moqui reservation, redesignated as a result of litigation) are an "island" within the Navajo lands.

Overnight accommodations are limited on the reservations; reserve rooms ahead or plan to stay at nearby communities or at the campgrounds along major reservation routes.

Always check on road conditions before venturing off the pavement. Keep a current road map at hand and carry water with you. For regulations and information, inquire at offices of the Navajo Rangers or Police.

When to go

This is high country, part of the vast Shonto Plateau. It is subject to snow in winter, unpaved roads turn into bogs during the thaws of early spring, and rains sometimes continue intermittently into May. However, the land is well drained. Unless there are washouts, roads usually become passable within hours after the storm blows over.

If you visit the region in spring, you have to gamble on the weather as you do on any spring trip into high country. March and early April often bring howling winds and dust

THE LAST HOLDOUTS in a drama of erosion, these majestic monoliths are still standing in Monument Valley long after the surrounding terrain has been eaten away by the elements.

AN ELECTRIFYING SPECTACLE at sundown, the striking buttes of Monument Valley are illuminated eerily by the rays of the late afternoon sun breaking through a blackening sky.

storms. You are likely to find the land at its very best from mid-April through May—grass tall and green on floors of the valleys, carpets of wildflowers, and spindle-legged spring lambs cavorting in the Navajo flocks.

Summer heat descends around mid-June, punctuated at fairly regular intervals by short, violent, traffic-stopping thunderstorms that continue through early September. Late September and October again bring ideal travel weather—warm, clear, sunshiny days and chill nights. By November, winter begins to close in.

THE NAVAJO RESERVATION

Four U.S. highways, roughly paralleling the boundaries of the reservation, provide access from its perimeter. Interstate 40, the major east-west route in Arizona, lies south of it between Flagstaff and Chambers, then cuts across its southeast corner near New Mexico. U.S. Highway 89, north-south between Page and Flagstaff, crosses the reservation for two-thirds of that distance. U.S. Highway 160 turns northeast from U.S. 89 north of Cameron and heads

for the Monument Valley and the Four Corners. In western New Mexico, U.S. Highway 666 between Gallup and Cortez, Colorado, crosses the reservation and is part of a direct route to the tribal capital at Window Rock. Window Rock is the major point of interest closest to the major travel route. Arizona Highway 264 goes east-west across the middle of the reservation and through the Hopi reservation.

The Navajos

As you travel the reservation, you will see evidence of the social and economic revolution that has been under way among the Navajos in recent years.

Ever since the Navajos signed a treaty in 1868 and returned home from four years of exile at Fort Sumner, New Mexico, their livelihood has depended principally on sheep-raising. But growth of the tribe and its herds increased the demands on the over-grazed range. The depression brought further miseries. By the end of World War II, a study of reservation resources warned that not more than half the tribe—even if its size remained the

HOW TO SHOP FOR INDIAN ART & HANDCRAFTS

Travelers to the Southwest have long been fascinated by the skill of Indian artists and craftsmen. Today, despite the quantity of mass-produced imitations on the market, fine Indian work is still being produced.

Studying quality Indian art is your best defense against imitations. Excellent museum displays can help train the eye and aid you in shopping wisely; museum gift shops are first-rate sources of authentic items. Indian art shows and displays at state, county, and tribal fairs across the Southwest offer both good shopping and the chance to meet Indian artists. Other reliable shopping sources are tribal-sponsored stores, artists' studios, and reputable galleries and shops.

Rugs. The Navajos, well-known for their beautiful handwoven rugs, learned weaving from the Pueblos, who rarely practice the art today. Use of native dyes or natural colors and fine, handspun yarn woven tightly gives these rugs the beauty and durability for which they are valued, but the long process required to achieve these qualities has limited the quantity of good rugs on the market. Check that the corners do not curl, that there are no wrinkles, and that edges are straight. Pry apart the fibers to check the warp—it should be wool, not cotton.

Pottery. Hopis and many Pueblo groups dominate pottery making, which is done by the ancient coil method rather than by a potter's wheel. In contrast to weaving, the ceramic arts are flourishing across the Southwest.

Prices reflect the size and quality of the object and the reputation of the artist. Rub your finger across the design on a pot; the paint shouldn't rub off.

Baskets. The time-consuming art of basket-weaving is concentrated among the Hopis and the Papagos; Hopi baskets are more scarce and more expensive. Quality of design and fineness of stitch determine price, and pieces that at first glance look similar actually may vary quite a bit. Inspect for firmness and evenness of weave before buying—some hasty, open-stitch work will dry and loosen.

Jewelry. The silver and turquoise jewelry of the Zunis, Navajos, and Hopis is popular, and some Indian silversmiths have expanded their craft to include such objects as hollowware, flatware, and small silver sculptures. Silver is the dominant element in the often massive Navajo jewelry; Zuni work emphasizes the stones and often includes shell, jet, and coral. Finely drawn overlay often characterizes Hopi silvercraft.

Reading the art. Designs on pottery, rugs, jewelry, and other objects are often purported to symbolize words or ideas. Listen to these stories with some skepticism; most designs serve the same function as those in abstract art.

The brightly colored Kachina dolls, though, do represent Hopi spirits, including about 250 individuals ranging from a ferocious black ogre who disciplines disobedient children to legendary figures from Hopi history.

KACHINA DOLLS represent Hopi spirits. Authentic dolls are carved from roots of live cottonwood trees and often labeled with the name of the spirit and name of the craftsman.

same—could be supported by the arid land. Fortunately, new sources of income were emerging. Uranium, oil, coal, and gas discoveries brought lease-bonus and royalty payments, and Congress voted long-range rehabilitation funds.

The Navajo Tribal Council began developing policies for economic diversification; it invested some of its income in job-creating tribal enterprises (irrigation projects, coal mining, forest products, arts and crafts outlets, tourist facilities) and encouraged private corporations to establish plants on reservation land. Tourism promotion particularly is now underway at a lively pace, and, in addition to working with outside tour operators, the tribe now offers its own tour packages and individually-tailored charter tours. The result of these efforts, with support from the Bureau of Indian Affairs, is a slow but steady broadening of the tribe's economic base.

Navajos have traditionally been semi-nomadic, following their flocks, living in simple hogans of logs and earth in winter and in simpler shade ramadas in summer. Seldom do you see more than two or three hogans together; the only towns on the Navajo reservation have grown up around governmental or industrial centers of employment.

But a new era in Navajo housing has begun. The traditional hogans are being replaced by small frame and concrete block houses; sometimes you see hogan and modern house side-by-side. Planned communities are growing around industrial and commercial developments, and many settlements are gradually taking on the appearance of any Southwestern crossroads cluster.

The Navajos' social revolution has been guided by their own political instrument, the Tribal Council. Along with citizenship in state and nation, the Navajo has a third political identity as a member of the tribe and helps elect a council with geographical representation.

Window Rock

This seat of tribal affairs gives dynamic evidence of the tribe's entrance into modern economic participation. The once sleepy crossroads on State 264 just west of the New Mexico border has turned into a busy intersection, where long lines of pickup trucks wait through two or three cycles of traffic signals to turn into the big parking lot of the metropolitan-style shopping center.

The road north still goes to the sandstone tribal headquarters. Buildings blend with the massive sandstone shapes around them; the large round window in the rock (for which the town was named) overlooks the complex. New permanent and prefabricated structures house burgeoning offices, and a large public library nestles next to a giant boulder.

West of the intersection on State 264 are the rodeo and fairgrounds, the civic center and Navajo Tribal Museum, and the visitor center and tourist information office housed in an old log building. The Window Rock Motor Inn and the showroom and work center of the Navajo Arts and Crafts Guild are east of the intersection on the state highway.

FORTRESSLIKE WALLS and startling sandstone spires rise from the desert in Canyon de Chelly.

By all means browse awhile in the Guild's display room. Even if you aren't planning to buy, you'll enjoy looking over the displays and comparing quality and prices. Much of the Navajos' best work is here: weaving, silver, leather, painting, and carving.

The Navajo Tribal Fair takes place at Window Rock in September—a lively celebration combining arts and crafts exhibits, an agricultural show, a rodeo, tribal ceremonials and carnival.

The Hubbell Trading Post

Don Lorenzo Hubbell founded his trading post at Ganado, at the crossing between State 264 and 63, in 1876, and it's still doing business in the old reservation tradition. Here the Navajos visit with friends and trade their wool, rugs, jewelry (and paychecks) for groceries and supplies. In the big warehouse next to the store, you'll see Navajo matrons weaving rugs. The establishment is now a National Historic Site. Rangers conduct daily guided tours of the post and the Hubbell home, which contains a fine collection of paintings and artifacts.

Canyon de Chelly

The Navajos call it *Tsegi,* "rock canyon." For more than 300 years, its fortresslike walls, rising to heights of more than a thousand feet, have provided a sanctuary against enemy forces that, at times, came to subdue or destroy the Navajo People.

Today, for many of the Navajos, the stubbornly preserved tribal heritage is being lost in the complexities of modern life; but Canyon de Chelly *(de shay)* still offers sanctuary to those who prefer the old ways. Each spring they return to plant their crops, tend their orchards, and graze their sheep in the quiet manner of their forefathers.

The entrance to the canyon is on Indian Route 7 just past the town of Chinle, a few miles east off State 63.

Park rangers conduct daily hikes into the canyon from the monument headquarters from about Memorial Day through Labor Day and present programs at the evening campfire in the public campground. Informal interpretive programs are given at most of the overlooks during the summer months. Inquire at monument headquarters for the day's programs. The headquarters museum offers unusually good exhibits on the history of the canyon and its inhabitants.

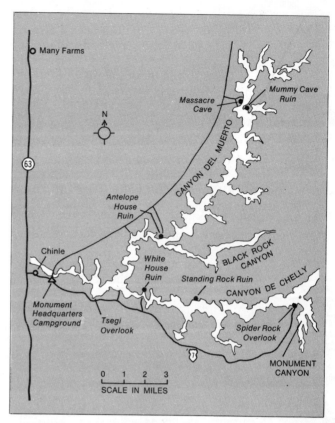

CANYON DE CHELLY is a box canyon offering hiking, riding tours, and spectacular scenery.

The Anasazi Ruins. Concern for the preservation of the ancient cliff dwellings of the *Anasazi* —"the ancient ones" who built their multistoried apartment houses in open caves along the canyon walls and on the canyon floor— caused the Federal Government to lease from the Navajo Tribe in 1931 about 130 square miles of the Canyon de Chelly-Canyon del Muerto complex as a national monument. The agreement stipulates that the administration of the area by the National Park Service will not interfere with the rights or privacy of the Navajo people who still live and farm here.

Visitors can follow a scenic drive along the south rim of the canyon to five spectacular overlooks, but, with one limited exception, visitors are not allowed within the canyons unless accompanied by an authorized guide. The exception is the mile-long hike from the canyon rim down to White House Ruin.

White House Ruin, the one most frequently seen by visitors, is typical of the 11th to 13th century cliff villages hidden in canyon caves throughout Arizona's red rock country. It's named for a long, white-plastered wall.

(Continued on next page)

Antelope Ruin, in tributary Canyon del Muerto 7 miles above its junction with Canyon de Chelly, is named for the large red-and-white antelope figures painted on the cliffs above it.

Mummy Cave Ruins, about 8 miles farther up Canyon del Muerto, is larger than the other two and once contained 90 rooms and 3 ceremonial kivas.

Where to stay. Accommodations, meals, and canyon tours in four-wheel-drive vehicles are available at Justin's Thunderbird Lodge near the mouth of Canyon de Chelly. (For information or reservations, write to Thunderbird Lodge, Box 548, Chinle, AZ 86503.)

Accommodations and food services are also available at nearby Chinle.

A 92-unit campground is located in a grove of tall cottonwood trees at the mouth of the canyon.

For more information on visitor services, write to Canyon de Chelly National Monument, Chinle, AZ 86503.

Monument Valley

The most famous section of the entire reservation, Monument Valley is a land of fantastic buttes and spires of rock rising from the desert. Now a Navajo Tribal Park, Monument Valley is northwest of Canyon de Chelly, astride the Arizona-Utah border on U.S. 163, which goes north from U.S. 160 at Kayenta.

Heading north from Kayenta, you first see the huge red rock pillars as you cross a crest after only a few minutes' driving. On your left are the Half Dome and Owl Rock promontories on the eastern edge of broad Tyende Mesa. On your right are isolated Burnt Foot Butte, then El Capitan. About 24 miles north of Kayenta, through the Mystery Valley with Wetherill Mesa on your right, you cross the Arizona-Utah border.

A half-mile north of the state line is a crossroads. To the left are Goulding's Trading Post and Lodge and Oljeto, site of a trading post and good air strip (the flying tours from Williams airport land here). To the right the road takes you to the Monument Valley visitor center. From the glass-walled observatory here you have excellent views of some of the better-known rock formations, the Mittens and Merrick Butte.

At the visitor center is a display and sales room of the Navajo Arts and Crafts Guild. A public campground is nearby.

You should not miss stopping at the visitor center. If you have more time, you can enter the park (the Navajos charge a small fee) and drive your own car on a 14-mile tour, staying on the marked roads but viewing the more famous landmarks: the tall, slender Three Sisters spires and the Totem Pole and Yiei Bichai group.

Tours. For deeper exploration, you can arrange for a guided tour in a four-wheel-drive vehicle; their operators are permitted to go beyond the marked roads.

These are tour operators: Goulding's, Kayenta, AZ 86033; Canyon Country Scenic Tours, Mexican Hat, Utah 84531; and Golden Sands Tours, Kayenta, AZ 86033. Navajo Scenic Tours at Window Rock also offers one-day tours.

Where to stay. Goulding's Lodge has long been a favorite. (For a long time it was the only place to stay.) Now there are excellent modern motels at Kayenta. Reservations are advised.

You can also reach the Monument Valley from U.S. 160 from Cortez, New Mexico, and U.S. 163 from Monticello, Utah.

Navajo National Monument

Another group of prehistoric cliff dwellings—Betatakin, Keet Seel, and Inscription House—is preserved in Navajo National Monument about 30 miles west of Kayenta. You can see Betatakin from monument headquarters, but it's a half-day tough hike to visit there (in guided groups only). You'll spend a day on a primitive trail, afoot or horseback, to reach Keet Seel, the largest cliff dwelling in Arizona. Inscription House, smallest of the three, is closed indefinitely for stabilization of the site.

You reach Navajo National Monument from U.S. Highway 160 about 30 miles west of Kayenta or 15 miles west of Tsegi. The turnoff at Black Mesa junction on State 564 takes you north 9 miles through juniper and piñon to the visitor center and Betatakin.

At the visitor center you'll find exhibits and a display room of the Navajo Arts and Crafts Guild. You'll find a traditional Navajo hogan and a small campground.

Betatakin. For a good view of Betatakin, take the easy walk (one mile round trip) from monument headquarters around the head of the box canyon and look across from the opposite rim.

The ancient apartment house is within a great cave in the canyon wall far below the headquarters building. To see it at close range, you must join a scheduled hiking group, limited to 20 persons, guided by a ranger. It's a three-hour round trip and a very tough climb back up. Don't try it if you're in poor shape or have heart problems.

Keet Seel. This ancient 160-room village, the largest cliff dwelling in Arizona, is 8 miles north of Betatakin by a canyon trail. From April through September, weather permitting, it's open to 25 visitors a day. But you must register a day ahead at monument headquarters. At that time you also can arrange to hire horses from the Navajos. If you're hiking, be prepared to splash across the stream several times.

To register in advance, to reserve horses, or to ask questions, write to the Superintendent, Navajo National Monument, Tonalea, AZ 86044, or telephone (602) 672-2366.

Inscription House. This ruin, 25 miles northwest, has suffered from visitor traffic and is closed for protection and repair. It will be reopened after stabilization; ask at headquarters.

The Four Corners

Up in the extreme northeast corner of Arizona, at the Navajo town of Teec Nos Pos, U.S. 160 turns north toward Four Corners where Arizona, New Mexico, Colorado, and Utah meet. Since it's the only place in the United States where that many state boundaries converge, the spot is marked with a tile-inlaid concrete slab.

U.S. 160 continues northeast toward Mesa Verde National Park in Colorado. At Teec Nos Pos, the east-west highway continues eastward as New Mexico Highway 504 to Shiprock, the giant rock sculpture that was a landmark to pioneers. There the state highway intersects with U.S. 666, the north-south route.

Tuba City

The principal town of the western half of the reservation is Tuba City, just north of the crossing between U.S. 160 and State 264. The large, white building is the Community Center, which the tribe uses for everything involving a crowd: committee meetings, medical clinics, movies, and dances. The Western Navajo Fair takes place in October with a rodeo and exhibits of arts and crafts .

Dinosaur tracks. Some 180 million years ago, this part of Arizona was an oozy mud flat where dinosaurs roamed. They left their footprints in the mud, which eventually hardened into rock, and you can see their tracks today.

The side road to the dinosaur tracks is a clearly-marked turnoff 5 miles west of Tuba City on U.S. 160. There's a small, waterless picnic area adjacent. Visitors also may picnic under shade trees near a small reservoir about 3 miles south on the same gravel road. Navajo Indians live nearby; their youngsters may be splashing in the reservoir.

The Little Colorado Gorge

West of the Cameron intersection, State 64 climbs through rolling hills toward the pine-forested highlands of the Grand Canyon's South Rim. There is sparse vegetation at first and much red dirt. You'll come across low, mesa-like formations topped by slabs of red sandstone, from which broken shards, like irregular garden flagstone, have fallen around the perimeter of these flat-topped hummocks.

Paralleling the highway on the north are the cliffs marking the gorge of the Little Colorado. The land is rising, and the gorge is deepening as the river moves to its confluence with the main stream in the Grand Canyon.

About 32 miles west of Cameron, the highway and the gorge converge at a spectacular overlook. Though the gorge here is not yet as deep as the Grand Canyon, it is much narrower, giving an impression of greater depth. From railed walks along the top of sheer cliffs, you peer straight down to the muddy river below, getting a foretaste of the Grand Canyon itself.

At the edge of the parking area, in good weather, Navajo matrons spread blankets to display beadwork and other jewelry for sale.

Navajo tours

From Window Rock, Navajo Scenic Tours operates tours of the reservation from May through September with Navajo guides, and including all transportation, lodging at first-class accommodations, and meals.

The 5 and 6-day package tours include Window Rock, Hubbell Trading Post, Canyon de Chelly, Wahweap and Glen Canyon, a boat cruise on Lake Powell, the Hopi villages, Navajo National Monument, and Monument Valley.

Available are special tours to selected attractions. For information, contact Navajo Scenic Tours, P.O. Box 809, Window Rock, Arizona 66515, or telephone (602) 871-4277.

THE HOPI RESERVATION

The Hopi Reservation is like the hole in a square doughnut, an enclave entirely surrounded by the vast Navajo lands. It lies astride Arizona Highway 264, about midway between north-south U.S. 89 on the west and north-south State 63 on the east.

The villages are clustered on the southern heights of three mesas. These the Hopis matter-of-factly call (east to west) First Mesa, Second Mesa, and Third Mesa. Actually, they are not individual mesas but three fingers of the giant Black Mesa reaching southwest from its long ridge.

The Hopi Agency is at Keams Canyon at the east end of the reservation on State 264, about 10 miles northwest of the intersection with State 77. At the trading post here, you can see good examples of a variety of Hopi artwork. You will find accommodations at the tribal-operated motel, the Hopituh trailer court, and a campground.

For information contact Hopi Tribal Headquarters, P.O. Box 123, New Oraibi, AZ 86039, or telephone (602) 734-2415.

The Hopis

Related culturally to the Pueblo people of northern New Mexico, the Hopis, unlike the Navajos, live in fixed locations. They have dwelt in their mesa-top villages for centuries. (Oraibi has been inhabited since about 1150, probably longer than any other community in the United States.)

Thus the villages are the focal points of Hopi affairs; and again unlike the Navajos, the Hopis have not developed a strong central tribal government, although they have a Tribal Council.

The Hopi reservation is completely surrounded by lands held jointly with the larger tribe and by the Navajo reservation itself.

From the time of their participation in the Pueblo Revolt of 1680 during which the Spanish were ejected from Indian lands, the Hopi people have remained independent from outside cultures. Later Spanish conquest did not include the Hopis, and most of the tribe today continues to resist the influence of modern civilization.

Their culture is extremely religious, and this is expressed in their complex calendar of colorful ceremonies. The most famous of these is the Snake Dance (climaxing many days of ceremonies in late August), during which the dancers carry live snakes in their mouths. The dances rotate between villages on alternate years; religious leaders of some villages have barred visitors during important ceremonies, including the Snake Dance.

From late December through the July "home dances," many other dances take place at which the participants impersonate the various Kachinas, the spiritual beings from the Hopi underground Heaven. Many of these are on weekends, but dates and places are not publicized and seeing them is usually a matter of luck. If you happen to be on the reservation, somebody at a shop or at the motel may mention the dance.

Once you get to a village where the dance is held, the Hopis will accept you graciously as long as you observe the ground rules: be unobtrusive and in no way interrupt or interfere with what's happening.

Cameras, recording equipment, and even sketch pads are strictly forbidden. If you have a camera, lock it up, out of sight in the car, before entering the village.

The colorfully costumed dancers, moving solemnly in a line to the muffled drumbeat, sometimes with mudheads or other clowns raising laughter from the understanding crowd, transform the drab villages.

The villages

At the base of First Mesa is the "modern" town of Polacca, built because of overflow from the traditional pueblo villages on top. To see the ancient settlements, you take a side road up the slope.

First Mesa villages are Shichumovi, Hano (not really a Hopi Village), and Walpi. Shichumovi and Hano merge together. In the late 17th century, a group of Tano Indians came here from New Mexico to flee the Spaniards, and the Hopis allowed them to settle. Walpi, on the point of the mesa, is considered the most picturesque. Its unpainted buildings, made of the same rock as the mesa, seem to grow out of the ground.

From Polacca, the highway climbs up the east side of Second Mesa, where side roads lead off to Shongopovi, Shipolovi, and Mishongnovi. Shongopovi alternates with Walpi in conducting the Snake Ceremonies—Shongopovi in even-numbered years, Walpi in odd years. Beside the highway on Second Mesa is the new Hopi Cultural Center.

On Third Mesa is Old Oraibi, the oldest continuously inhabited settlement in the United

WEATHERED FACE of towering cliff rises above a side-canyon beach on Lake Powell.

States, having been established in 1150 A.D. It was once the largest of the Hopi villages, but its population has dwindled and many of the buildings are abandoned. Younger villages are Bacavi and Hotvilla founded in this century. At the foot of the mesa is New Oraibi, founded by Hopis who had been converted to Christianity. The Tribal Council headquarters is here.

On the banks of the washes and in the flats below the mesas, the Hopis cultivate their crops: many varieties of corn, squash, melons, and beans. Peach orchards produce small fruit that is dried in the sun.

The mesa-top villages may seem desolate; they're dry, treeless, sunbaked. When there's not a dance, there's very little to attract visitors off the highway. Usually you'll be treated politely, and somebody will approach and ask if you need help with something (it may be the village policeman, although this will not be evident by his appearance). The villages really are not public places, and visitors are few except for those on guided tours.

The Cultural Center

Beside the highway on Second Mesa is the Hopi Cultural Center, a complex of motel, museum, restaurant, and shops. The center is handsome, its austere style harmonizing with the angular landscape and native structures.

The motel has very comfortable rooms (no TV, no telephones; but nobody has complained). The museum has excellent displays of Hopi historical relics and crafts. As in the villages, photography is not permitted. One of the shops is the outlet of Hopicrafts, representing a group of top-ranking craftsmen.

The studio, gallery, and sales room of the Hopi Arts & Crafts Silvercraft Cooperative Guild (where you can see and buy excellent silverwork, weaving, pottery, basketry, Kachina dolls, and paintings) is directly west of the Cultural Center. You may see Hopi silversmiths creating their distinctive overlay jewelry in a shop adjacent to the showroom.

GLEN CANYON NATIONAL RECREATION AREA

The Navajo Reservation extends across the Arizona-Utah border to the southern boundary of the Glen Canyon National Recreation Area. The Recreation Area encloses 186-mile-long Lake Powell, created by Glen Canyon Dam on the Colorado River. The area headquarters is at

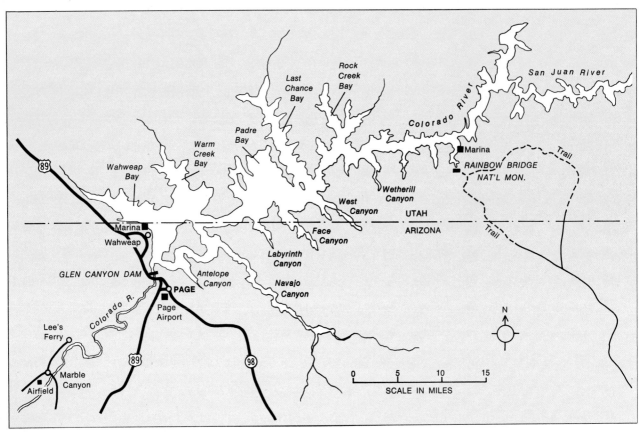

SPANNING Arizona and Utah border, Glen Canyon National Recreation Area was a secluded canyon of the Colorado; area is excellent for fishing, boating, camping and canyon exploring.

Page, Arizona, the town that was born of the construction boom and has remained as a tourist center. The tremendous lake and the now-broadened Colorado and San Juan rivers extend into the southeast corner of Utah.

Glen Canyon Dam and visitor center

U.S. 89 spans the Colorado River on a steel arch below the dam, overlooking the barrier and the broad expanse of the lake. Completed in 1964, the dam rises 710 feet above bedrock, 583 feet above the original river channel, and is 1,560 feet across at the crest. You get a fine view of it from the walkway on the bridge. At the west end, on the canyon rim, the Carl Hayden Visitor Center has displays and information about the dam and lake and is the starting point for tours of the dam. It's open daily; check for the hours.

Wahweap

Wahweap, 4½ miles north of the dam on the west side, features a swimming beach, a large marina, trailer and camper village with utility hookups, a lodge and motel, and a Park Service campground with 178 campsites. Bring your own firewood or fuel for the camp. Here also are the district ranger's office of the Park Service and the headquarters of Canyon Tours, the concessioner who operates the marina, tours, and boat rentals, including houseboats. There are boat-in campsites and marinas along the lake shores.

The boat tours range from one-hour trips near the dam to five-day trips that combine hikes and overland expeditions.

Information and reservations

Because Lake Powell has become a very popular tourist attraction, reservations are advised. For accommodations at Wahweap, boat rentals, and tours, write Canyon Tours, Inc., Box 1597, Page, AZ 86040, or phone (602) 645-2448.

For information about the area and Park Service facilities, write to the Superintendent, Glen Canyon National Recreation Area, Box 1507, Page, AZ 86040.

ABOVE, *curving wake of boat laps sheer red sandstone walls of Reflection Canyon.*

BOATING is best way to see Lake Powell's twisting shoreline. Wahweap Marina (above) is a popular starting point. Narrow canyon (right) is one of hundreds of side canyons to explore by boat.

GRACEFUL *arch spans Rainbow Canyon.*

The Phoenix area

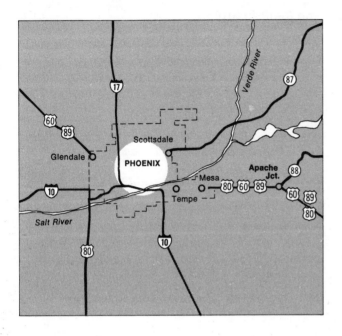

Why here, of all places? What is this vigorous, metropolitan complex, the biggest inland city in the Pacific Southwest, doing here in the middle of the desert? It's the water.

The Salt River emerges from the Superstition and Mazatzal Mountains east of the city, joins the Verde River waters from the Coconino and Mogollon plateaus, and winds westward across this desert to join the Gila River a few miles west. Phoenix was born on the river, grew astride it, and is still growing.

The river doesn't look impressive as you cross its wide, sandy bed to Tempe or Mesa. There's no water during much of the year; it's all stored behind the dams up in the canyons along the Apache Trail or sliding smoothly down the canals that fan out across the valley.

Phoenix today is a commercial and manufacturing center, but it started as a farm town living on that water. This lower Salt River

DESERT METROPOLIS of Phoenix spreads over lower Salt River Valley below South Mountain Park.

Valley is still one of the richest agricultural sites in the Southwest, thanks to waters stored in a chain of manmade lakes—Saguaro, Canyon, and Apache on the Salt; Bartlett and Horseshoe on the Verde—and doled out for irrigation year round. This vast Salt River Project was America's first major reclamation effort.

The best way to understand it all is to see a relief model of the valleys, surrounding mountains, and system of waterways that have created the oasis. You will find such a model in the terminal building at Sky Harbor Airport (where you'll also see a dramatic mural depicting that mythical bird, the phoenix, which rose from its own ashes—as this city of Phoenix has risen on the ruins of the ancient civilization of the vanished Hohokam). Or look at the relief map of Arizona in the Valley National Bank, 141 N. Central Avenue.

When to come

The fine weather comes to the Valley of the Sun about October and lasts into May. But traditionally the heavy influx of visitors comes after Christmas and stays until Easter. Because of this pattern, the early and late portions of the season usually offer lower rates and less crowded accommodations. For three or four months of the year, Phoenix is hot (though, mercifully, the humidity is low). Yet so universal has air conditioning become in the valley that publicists advertise Phoenix as the "year round vacation capital" with some justification.

Where to stay

With a reasonable amount of advance planning, you should not have difficulty getting reservations, even for a visit at the height of the season, for accommodations are plentiful.

For a comprehensive list of accommodations in Phoenix and the surrounding area, write to Phoenix & Valley of the Sun Convention & Visitors Bureau, 2701 E. Camelback Road, Suite 200H, Phoenix, AZ 85016, or call (602) 957-0070.

For a 24-hour recording of current events in the area, call (602) 956-6200. Information can also be obtained at the visitors' booth at Sky Harbor Airport.

What to do

Phoenix and the surrounding countryside offer countless opportunities for recreation. The Phoenix Parks and Recreation Department, the Maricopa County Parks and Recreation Department, and various valley communities provide a wide range of activities for residents and visitors of all ages. Excellent nature walks, for example, are sponsored by the county department. To obtain specific information, write or telephone the department concerned.

Horseback riding. Regional parks and open country provide the best opportunities to confront the desert on horseback. The banks of all 130 miles of the Salt River Project's canals are closed to private vehicles and motorcycles and are open to horseback riders. A bridle path, pleasantly shaded by a canopy of arching trees, parallels North Central Avenue for several miles north of Bethany Home Road.

In winter the Maricopa County Parks and Recreation Department sponsors monthly trail rides to regional parks. For addresses of rental stables, see the yellow pages of the local telephone directory. Many resorts maintain their own stables.

Golf. For those who are in search of a "dogleg to the right," the Phoenix area abounds in opportunities. The terrain is marked with the rolling fairways of more than 60 golf courses.

Tennis. You will find courts at parks, playgrounds, schools, clubs, and resorts for this year-round sport.

Boating and water-skiing. The many man-made lakes provide excellent sites for these popular water activities. You can rent boats and motors at Lake Pleasant (lower lake is closed to motors) and at all four Salt River lakes. Saguaro Lake is the closest of these, reached from State Highway 87.

Fishing. Phoenix's lakes yield bass, bluegill, channel catfish, and crappie. The canals, too, often reward the patient angler. Licenses are sold at sporting goods stores.

Hiking and camping. With a good pair of walking shoes, some drinking water, and a hat, you can take advantage of many miles of hiking trails. The banks of the Salt River Project's irrigation canals are all good hiking areas. Or acquaint yourself with the life of the desert while camping in one of the Maricopa County regional parks or in the Tonto National Forest.

A list of the Forest Service recreational facilities is available from the Supervisor, Tonto National Forest, Federal Building, First Avenue and Monroe Street.

Bicycle trips. In Phoenix and the adjacent desert, the Arizona Bicycle Club, 4420 E. Taylor, Phoenix, AZ 85008, organizes weekend rides. Trip variations are geared to the stamina of the riders. Beginners take relatively short jaunts along the canals; intermediate cyclers might ride out to Taliesin West; and practiced riders go on expeditions as far as Tucson.

Surfing. At Big Surf, in the middle of the desert, the surf's up, and you don't have to worry about the tides. On a large freshwater lagoon you ride rolling breakers up to five feet high, created by a hydraulic wave maker. The waves roll onto a palm-dotted, four-acre, sandy beach. For information about the season, hours, and admission prices, write Big Surf, P.O. Box L, 1500 N. Hayden Road, Tempe 85281, or telephone 947-2477.

Ice skating. If warm temperatures start to get to you, give your air conditioner a rest and head for one of the city's four ice skating rinks: Ice Palace East, 3853 E. Thomas Road; Ice Palace West, 2740 W. Indian School Road; Ice Capades Chalet at Metrocenter, west of Black Canyon Freeway; or Oceanside Ice Arena, 1520 N. Hayden Road, Tempe.

For the spectator

Since the valley is alive with activity from fall to spring, the following is only a sampling. For a more complete listing and specific dates, contact the Phoenix & Valley of the Sun Convention & Visitors Bureau at the address on page 51.

Major league baseball. The valley has long been a spring training locale for major league baseball teams including, in recent years, the San Francisco Giants, Chicago Clubs, Milwaukee Brewers, the Oakland Athletics, and the Seattle Mariners.

Tennis tournament. The Phoenix Thunderbird Tennis Tournament is held in March at the Phoenix Country Club.

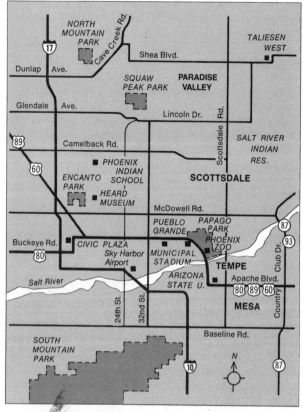

DOWNTOWN PHOENIX is dotted with many attractions for participant as well as spectator.

Golf tournament. Among the 75 tournaments held each year, you can catch the top pros in the act during the Phoenix Open in January and the Arizona Open in November.

Horse racing. Turf Paradise track operates from mid-November to February, and the horses run at Arizona Downs from February to mid-April. Racing days are Wednesdays, Fridays, Saturdays, Sundays, and holidays.

Greyhound racing. In Phoenix races are held at Phoenix, Apache, and Black Canyon greyhound parks from January to April and from mid-September to mid-December, Tuesday through Sunday nights.

Rodeos. The annual Phoenix "Rodeo of Rodeos," during March in the Memorial Coliseum at the Arizona State Fairgrounds is one of the contests on which the cowboys' world championships are based. You see top ropers, riders, and bull-doggers pitted against tough, fresh rodeo stock.

Scottsdale's colorful Parada del Sol takes place in early February at the Scottsdale Rodeo Grounds.

Small rodeos often take place within easy driving distance of Phoenix in winter and spring.

Horse shows, gymkhanas. Some of the world's finest Arabian horses compete in the All-Arabian Horse Show in February at Paradise Park, Scottsdale. The A-Z (Aid to the Zoo) National Horse Show is in March at Memorial Coliseum. In March the Western Saddle Club holds an annual Stampede at the club arena, 18th Street and Myrtle Avenue.

Livestock show. You can attend the Arizona National Livestock Show in early January at the State Fairgrounds.

Cactus show. Examine the plants of the desert during the annual Cactus Show held in February at the Desert Botanical Garden in Papago Park.

Dons club. Every winter this business and professional men's organization hosts a series of weekend tours to points of interest throughout the state. Tours are by bus, although you can tag along behind in your own car on one-day outings. Annual highlight is the Lost Dutchman Gold Mine Trek into the Superstitions in early March. (For a complete schedule, write to Box 13493, Phoenix AZ 85002.)

Plays and concerts. There's a lively agenda of musical and theatrical events in the valley. In Phoenix, the curtain rises on productions by the Phoenix Little Theater at Phoenix Civic Center; Celebrity Theater (in the round) at 32nd Street and Van Buren; Phoenix Theater for the Performing Arts, 1202 North Third Street; and the Black Theater Troup, 1002 East Monroe. The Phoenix Symphony Orchestra has a hall in the Civic Plaza for its performances, and it's one of the handsomest of such facilities in the country.

Scottsdale has its Chamber Opera, Musical Comedy Theater, Sagebrush Theater, and Center for the Arts. In Tempe, events are scheduled frequently at the Center for the Performing Arts at the University of Arizona.

IN THE CITY

Phoenix is a city of contrasts—a modern sprawling metropolis dotted with attractive parks and bits of history taking you hundreds of years back in time. Sights range from the ever-present Camelback Mountain northeast of the city (from the city the mountain looks like a camel in repose) to the spectacular flower fields along

Baseline Road, south of the Salt River, where brightly colored carnations, sweet peas, calendulas, and stock put on an annual show from late January until just before Easter.

Phoenix Civic Plaza

This ultra-modern "people place," lighted spectacularly at night, includes a concert hall-theater, complete convention center complex, and landscaped plaza, providing an oasis in the center of the city.

The entire complex covers six former city blocks with a parking garage beneath. Check the events scheduled there during your visit.

Museums

A variety of excellent museums in the city tells much of the story of Phoenix, Arizona, and the Southwest. Exhibits testify to the turbulent history of the area, the geologic make-up of the land, and the culture of its people.

Heard Museum. Exhibits in this museum of anthropology and primitive art focus on the art of American Indians, with special emphasis on the tribes of the Southwest. Other exhibits include works of contemporary Indian artists and craftsmen.

The most complete collection of Hopi and Zuni Kachina dolls in the world is housed in the museum, and a changing exhibit of them is on display in the Kachina Gallery of the museum. These brightly colored representatives of Kachina spirits are imitated for many curio shops, but this gallery offers an opportunity to study the real thing.

The liveliest weekend of the year at the museum is the annual spring Indian Fair. Representatives of a dozen or more tribes gather on the museum grounds to present their finest artists, craftsmen, musicians, and dancers. You can watch Papago basketmakers coil drab strands of yucca fiber into boldly decorative baskets and plaques, see skilled Pueblo potters transform their clay into exquisite vessels, or sample freshly made piki bread. The colorful dance programs offer photographers a chance to record the rituals and costumes of tribes that restrict cameras on the reservation.

In April there's a lecture or presentation on regional history or Indian cultures. Newspapers carry the announcements.

In fall the Indian Arts and Crafts Exhibit has displays of Indian articles submitted for competition. All are for sale but must remain on exhibit until the close of the show.

The museum at 22 E. Monte Vista Road is open all day Monday through Saturday, and in the afternoon on Sundays.

Mineral Museum. Residents and visitors alike find the Arizona Mineral Museum a fascinating storehouse of minerals, rocks, and semiprecious stones. Among the displays are a fossilized mammoth tooth, a meteorite, and one of the world's largest quartz crystals.

Arizona is the nation's leading copper producer; extensive exhibits trace the state's mining industry from early discoveries to present day technology.

The museum is in the southwest corner of the Arizona State Fairgrounds at McDowell Road and North 19th Avenue. It's open mornings and afternoons daily and on weekend afternoons; admission is free.

A wax museum. You can picture yourself pitted in a violent gun battle of the Old West or swapping yarns with some of the most famous good guys and bad guys as you wander through the exhibits at the Royal London Wax Museum. The museum, depicting scenes of the Old West, is near Papago Park at 5555 East Van Buren. There is an admission fee.

Phoenix Art Museum. A part of the Civic Center on N. Central Avenue houses this diverse collection of painting and sculpture. The museum is open all day Tuesday through Saturday and in the afternoon on Sunday. Admission is free.

History Room. Displays of early Arizona history occupy this room of the First National Bank of Arizona. The room is open during regular banking hours at 100 W. Washington; admission is free. Exhibits are changed periodically.

Arizona Museum. Relics of Arizona pioneer days, pieces of Indian art, and historic maps are among the displays here. The museum at 10th Avenue and West Van Buren is open Wednesday through Sunday from 2 to 5 p.m. November to June; admission is free.

A telephone museum. Phoenix's smallest museum and one of its more interesting is operated by the Coronado Chapter of the Telephone Pioneers of America. Located in a narrow room of Mountain States Telephone Company's administration building at 16 W. McDowell Road, it displays more than 70 telephones (the oldest made in 1887), eight switchboards, and many other pieces of equipment associated with wire communication. The museum is open to visitors during business hours.

OUTDOOR SPORTS are a way of life in the Valley of the Sun. Riders above are exploring the countryside near Scottsdale. At Big Surf, below, raft-riding on manmade waves thrills youngsters.

The native American

Much of the character of the Southwest can be attributed to its native inhabitants, the Indians. Few places afford the opportunity to study the development of the Indian tribes from the past to the present the way this region of the country does. A number of attractions around Phoenix offer insight into Indian history; some reveal tribal life today. In the city there are two such attractions: Pueblo Grande and the Phoenix Indian School.

Pueblo Grande. Excavations at this 13th century village ruin have provided much of our knowledge about the valley's former residents, master farmers who created such an efficient irrigation system that 20th century engineers followed their courses for the present canals. The Hohokam abandoned this village and the Casa Grande (see page 60) before the white man came. Pueblo Grande is at 4619 E. Washington Street. Hours are 1 to 4:30 p.m. Sunday and holidays, and 9 to 4:30 Monday through Friday. Admission is free.

Phoenix Indian School. One of the Southwest's oldest and largest Indian boarding schools is located at North Central Avenue and Indian School Road. The majority of students—who number more than 1,000—come from the Hopi, Papago, Navajo, Pima, Apache, and Colorado River reservations; a total of 20 tribes are represented. At this school run by the Bureau of Indian Affairs, visitors are welcome on Fridays from 9 to 11 and 1 to 3.

City parks

Within its city limits Phoenix has a gem of a metropolitan park, three rugged near-wilderness preserves, and one area that combines natural terrain features with developed facilities.

Encanto Park. The downtown park at Encanto Boulevard and 15th Avenue is a favorite sports and recreation area with free admission. Its 200-acre area includes a lagoon with boats for hire. The park offers facilities for golf (two courses), tennis, swimming, badminton, shuffleboard, and picnicking. There are also rides and amusements for children, a band shell, wide expanses of lawn, a garden center, and walks leading through handsome and varied plantings of trees and shrubs.

Papago Park. This combined urban and natural desert park at the eastern city limits offers picnicking, hiking, an 11.3-mile bike trail, horseback riding (rental stables are nearby), an 18-hole golf course, the municipal stadium (home of the Phoenix Giants, spring training park for the San Francisco Giants), seven small lakes where youngsters 15 and under may fish without licenses, the famed Desert Botanical Garden, and the Phoenix Zoo and Children's Zoo. There's no fee to enter the park itself.

Desert Botanical Garden. For a good introduction to desert plant life (both native and non-native), this garden contains an enormous array of cactus and succulents. Other tradi-

Saguaro

Nama demissum & Monoptilon bellioides

Hibiscus denudatus

Yucca elata

tional plants you'll see include palo verde, ironwood, mesquite trees, and ocotillo. Stop at the visitor's building to buy a 10-cent booklet, *Self Conducted Nature Walk*, that tells what you see as you walk through the gardens. The pamphlet includes a plant-by-plant description covering the botanical name, history, kind of fruit, blooming time, maximum height, and other interesting facts on each plant. The garden is open daily. There's a small entrance fee.

Phoenix Zoo. One of the most appealing attractions in the valley for children and adults alike, the zoo has an impressive collection of animals. Here is the only breeding herd in captivity of Arabian oryx, the gazelle-like creature whose long, straight, parallel horns, seen in profile, started the myth of the unicorn. Hunted to near extinction, the species' survival may depend upon these 28 animals sent here by Saudi Arabian officials because of the similar climate.

A special feature is the Children's Zoo, where youngsters can pet and feed small animals, see a barnyard menagerie including Texas longhorn steers, and visit the brooder house to see the development of baby chicks from hatching to five weeks old. Another feature the youngsters will like is the trained animal show—lions, tigers, chimps—every morning but Monday and Tuesday and twice on weekend afternoons.

The zoo is open daily; if you're inside by 5, you can stay until sunset.

South Mountain Park. For a picnic or a hike, you can't beat the biggest municipal park in the world. Almost 15,000 acres of mostly wilderness, it includes improved picnic sites, 40 miles of hiking and bridle trails (rental stables), and a paved scenic drive to two vantage points from which you have sweeping views of the Salt and Gila River valleys. Pedestrians are admitted free, but there's a small charge for vehicles.

North Mountain Park. Far across Phoenix at the north end of Central Avenue (enter from 10600 North Seventh Street), a small but popular destination for picnickers, hikers, and riders (there's no stable) beckons. The grounds include five picnic areas and a children's playground. The ranger's office houses a collection of desert insects and Indian artifacts. No fee.

Squaw Peak Park. The peak itself is a good hike. Ramadas of various sizes accommodate picnickers at this park north of the city. No fee.

To reserve ramadas for picnics at Papago Park, North Mountain, or Squaw Peak, phone

Ocotillo

Mesquite

Mammillaria

Encelia farinosa

Euphorbia albomarginata

Hedgehog cactus

ROCK CARVINGS in Estrella Mountains southwest of Phoenix have withstood centuries of weathering.

SUCCESSFUL fishermen reel in white bass from popular Lake Pleasant.

262-6711. For a South Mountain picnic reservation, phone 276-2221.

Legend City. In this family recreation park, you can choose among 53 acres of such attractions as a ghost town, a river boat ride, and a replica of the Lost Dutchman Mine. Call the park, on the Phoenix-Tempe city limits, for hours and admission prices: 275-8551.

OUTSIDE PHOENIX

The outlying area around Phoenix contains a potpourri of inviting attractions, all within an easy drive of the city. You can enjoy the rugged and serene beauty of the desert, relax and have a picnic, or try your hand at boating in one of the regional parks. A fascinating aspect of this region is the constant presence of history visible through the remains of the dwellings of early civilizations. You cover a 600 year span in time as you travel from the ancient ruins of Casa Grande to the futuristic studio of Paolo Soleri.

Scottsdale

A lively resort center just east of Phoenix, Scottsdale is self-styled as "the West's most

Western town" and is probably also the West's most growing town, already the third largest in the state. Western style outdoor living and the garb of the western rider—levis, boots, and cowboy hat—set the theme, although the town also boasts 15 golf courses and 45 tennis courts.

The Civic Center. Scottsdale's handsome Civic Center (city hall and library) designed by architect Bennie Gonzales, suggests the Spanish Morocco style in its clean, monolithic lines. Sunlight streaming through stained glass windows paints interior walls with color. Dale Wright's welded steel sculpture of Don Quixote rises from the pool fronting the complex; John Waddell's *Mother and Child* and the abstract Children's Fountain are nearby.

Scottsdale Mall. Between the Civic Center and Brown Avenue, shops, galleries, restaurants, cinemas, and a hotel occupy buildings around 20-acre, parklike Scottsdale Mall. Adjacent to the Mall, the Center for the Arts features changing art exhibits as well as theatrical, musical, and film productions.

Old Town. A touch of the Old West, Old Town (downtown Scottsdale) has streets lined with carefully preserved frontier buildings resembling Western movie sets. Situated between 68th Street and Bronson Avenue, Second Street and Indian School Road, Old Town is a great place to shop for Western goodies: new duds, an Indian rug, or pottery. The work of Western artists fills several galleries.

Fifth Avenue. In the Fifth Avenue shopping area many fine shops specialize in the unusual. "Craftsmen's Court" (Kiva Plaza) is a landscaped courtyard with benches where tired shoppers can take a welcome rest in the shade. Perfumed water splashes from a fountain; sheltered doorways lead to intriguing small shops.

Paolo Soleri's studio. On display at the studio are models and full-size concrete structures expressing this unorthodox designer's ideas for future housing. A small donation admits visitors to workshops and exhibits, open daily. The studio is on Double Tree Road, about a mile west of Scottsdale Road.

Taliesen West. The western campus of the Frank Lloyd Wright School of Architecture east of Scottsdale is living expression of the great architect's building and landscape designs. His concepts are kept alive and in continual growth by his associates and students. As part of their training, students plan and build additions and maintain the buildings and gardens that flow together in harmony.

The campus is open to visitors year round, although the faculty and students move to the original Taliesen near Green Spring, Wisconsin, during the summer months.

Visitors' hours are 10 to 4 daily, 12 to 4 Sunday, and may occasionally be changed. There is an admission fee. Follow the signs off Shea Boulevard north on 108th Street.

Fountain Hills. Driving east of Scottsdale past the McDowell Mountains on Shea Boulevard, the traveler encounters a strange sight in the desert. Rising from a large lagoon in the plush residential development of Fountain Hills, a tall plume of water claims the record for the world's highest fountain (560 feet) when the three pumps work at full power. A 2,000-pound nozzle constricts water flowing at 7,000 gallons per minute, keeping eight tons of water suspended in the air.

To the foothills

North of the city, Scottsdale Road leads to Carefree and Cave Creek, uncrowded and scenic residential communities in the foothills. En-route, the road passes places of interest, and a turnoff on Pinnacle Peak Road takes you to a panoramic view of the city. A popular stop on this road is Pinnacle Peak Patio, a huge steakhouse famed for its custom of cutting off the neckties of those who defy the "no tie" rule. Thousands of these ties cover the ceiling.

Rawhide. A ring of Conestoga wagons beside the road greets visitors to this replica of an 1880s town. Lining the dusty street are craft shops, a period barber shop, a cavernous saloon and restaurant featuring cowboy steaks, a reconstructed "Arizona's first bank," sheriff's office, general store, museum (Geronimo's moccasins, Tom Mix's boots), livery stable, gem display, and, at the end, a mine shaft and ore car. You can pan gold nearby, take a stagecoach ride, and watch a frontier blacksmith at work.

Rawhide is open from 5 p.m. to midnight Monday through Friday, noon to midnight Saturday and Sunday. Admission is free.

Southwestern Studio. Here you can tour studios and sets where TV series, features, and commercials are produced. An expert who is literally the fastest gun in the world lectures on production techniques and special effects. Open Wednesday through Sunday from 11 a.m. to 5 p.m. October through April, the studio on Scottsdale Road is only open on weekends from May to September. There's a small fee for the 50-minute tour.

Carefree. A colorful Spanish village of red tile roofs on white stuccoed shops clusters around a large, flower-filled patio. Like Scottsdale's Craftsmen's Court, the shaded patio invites a pause. Carefree also boasts "the world's largest sundial."

Cave Creek. Over the hill and around the bend to the west of Carefree, another residential settlement has controlled development and preserved the open space and charm of the desert foothills. Harold's, a bar and steakhouse, provides local color. On rare wet days, the rain falls almost as hard under the roof as outside this rambling, ramshackle landmark.

The center of dude ranching in the area, Cave Creek is the takeoff point for the wilderness recreation area to the west. From Carefree a paved road takes you about 14 miles northeast into the Camp Creek canyon and campsites. Here the pavement ends, but the gravel road continues a scenic 50-mile loop north through the mountains past Seven Springs, Cedar Mountain, and Brooklyn Mountain to meet Interstate 17 north of Bumble Bee.

Desert foothills scenic drive. This drive reveals the energy and foresight of concerned citizens of Cave Creek and Carefree. Anxious to preserve the choice desert you will see at roadside, they realized it would be more meaningful —and less prone to damage—if those who passed along the road were acquainted with the individual plants. So they identified 26 species and erected 101 roadside signs to mark them. Some plants are visible from the road; to see others requires a short walk.

A naturalist, aided by students and faculty members of Arizona State University, located and identified the plants to be marked. Residents built, carved, and painted the signs, using materials contributed by a lumber yard. School children helped clean up the sites and install the signs. Families adopted individual plants and assumed responsibility for their care.

Exhibits are repeated so that either way you approach the loop you may see all the specimens. For a pleasant day's drive out of Phoenix, start at Scottsdale in the morning for browsing and lunch; then make the tour north through Carefree and Cave Creek in the afternoon. Watch the sunset from the Cave Creek Road as you return to Phoenix.

Some Arizona landmarks

Much of the fascination of the Southwest lies in contrast—the omnipresent signs of the past and their proximity to the most modern developments. The area around Phoenix offers a variety of these sights, starting with the silent ruins of Casa Grande, continuing through the Indian blend of early and modern cultures, and looking into the future with jet aircraft and Arizona State University. All provide a chapter in the continuing chronicle of the Southwest; all are short drives from the center of Phoenix.

Casa Grande Ruins National Monument. Here you will see a strange structure rearing out of the desert: a four-story tower built 600 years ago by Pueblo and Hohokam Indian farmers of the Gila Valley. The tower served as lookout, fort, and 11-room, 11-family apartment house. Padre Kino named it the Casa Grande when he discovered it in 1694. Today, sheltered by a steel canopy, the "large house" is the central feature of the monument. A ranger will take you through the building; there is a guide service every day from 8 a.m. to 5 p.m. (a small fee is charged).

You can see other evidence of the Hohokam in the irrigation canals and walled-in village ruins on the monument grounds. A museum at monument headquarters displays artifacts excavated from six village compounds. Visitors may picnic in a shaded area provided with water and tables.

Signs on Interstate 10 mark the turnoff about 40 miles south of Phoenix.

St. John's Indian School. Widely known for its colorful ceremonial dancers and drum and bugle corps who appear in festivals and parades throughout the Southwest, the school is an adjunct of the Franciscan mission at the village of Komatke on the Gila River Indian Reservation. In addition to Pimas and Maricopas from the local reservation, the school attracts students from as far as the Pacific Northwest. Visitors are welcomed during the school year, but telephone 276-8500 in advance for arrangements. To reach the mission, about 16 miles southwest of the city, turn south on 51st Avenue through Laveen, and follow the signs.

Sacaton. To visit the Pima agency town and headquarters of the Gila River Indian Reservation, drive about 40 miles south of Phoenix. These days the Pimas rarely make the tightly coiled baskets for which they are famous; most farm on the reservation or work in town.

Early rock carvings are found at a number of places on the reservation. A site with hundreds of these petroglyphs lies in a canyon just outside the old trading post of Oldberg, reached by a road from Highway 87 east of Sacaton.

Guadalupe. Yaqui Indians settled at this small village southeast of Phoenix after fleeing from Mexico and continue to maintain a somewhat separate culture here. Their celebration of Easter, combining Christian and pre-Colombian elements, attracts interest. The village sits at the northeast tip of South Mountain Park.

Pioneer Arizona. The Southwestern counterpart of the "living history museum" at Williamsburg, Virginia, has been created on 550 acres north of Phoenix. Costumed guides demonstrate realistic daily activities in authentically restored buildings.

Pioneer Arizona is open daily until sunset. Expect a small admission fee. Watch for signs on Interstate 17 about five miles south of New River.

Arizona State University. On a visit to the modern, beautifully landscaped campus in Tempe, check the schedule of events at the Center for the Performing Arts, the University auditorium designed by Frank Lloyd Wright. In Matthews Center you can also view the permanent Collection of American Art, which provides the mainstay for continually rotating art exhibits.

Mormon Temple. The Temple's formally landscaped grounds are open to the public, but the building itself, one of the largest in the country, is open only to Mormons. The Temple is near the center of the town of Mesa.

Regional parks

Though Phoenix is one of the most rapidly growing cities in the West, its planners have taken care to preserve a valuable commodity —open space. Residents of Phoenix and the rest of Maricopa County enjoy one of the largest systems of regional parks in the country; they cover some 94,000 acres. You will find that much of this land was kept in its original wilderness state, unaltered by prior development.

All of these dry desert parks can be very pleasant from February through April when desert flowers bloom, but May brings the be-

ginning of hot weather along with the cactus flowers. For more information, contact the Maricopa County Parks and Recreation Department, 4701 East Washington Street, Phoenix, AZ 85032, or phone 262-3711.

Lake Pleasant Regional Park. The most developed of the parks, this one has paved access roads, shaded picnic areas, swimming beach, launching ramps, docks, fueling dock, and overnight campgrounds. Water sports, fishing, and rock hunting are popular here.

Black Canyon Recreation Area. If you're interested in perfecting your marksmanship, plan a stop at this recreation area on Interstate 17. Shooting ranges include small bore, big bore, skeet, trap, and archery. Non-shooters will enjoy good picnic facilities.

Cave Creek Recreation Area. This undeveloped park east of Interstate 17 affords good riding, hiking, and overnight camping. Bring your own water and campstove.

McDowell Mountain Regional Park. A refuge for wildlife next to the Fort McDowell Indian Reservation, this park is popular for riding, hiking, picnicking, and camping. Access is by gravel roads; bring water.

The adjacent reservation straddles the Verde River where Shea Boulevard meets Highway 87. Some Apache Indians live and farm here.

Usery Mountain Park. This well-developed park has picnic tables, an archery range, and a campground. There is no water.

Estrella Mountain Regional Park. This big mountain refuge for wildlife and people is adjacent to the Casey Abbott Recreational Area and has developed picnic areas (including water), overnight camping units, an archery range, and a nearby 18-hole golf course. Riding and hiking trails lead into the mountains.

Buckeye Hills Recreation Area. You can enjoy riding, hiking, and camping at another desert hills sanctuary. There are picnic sites and a small shooting range, but again, no water.

White Tank Mountain Regional Park. The largest of the ring of parks, this one has picnic tables, a campground, and marked hiking trails. No water.

Thunderbird Recreation Area. This park is closer in and offers hiking and picnicking. Drinking water is available.

RING of regional parks preserves natural open space and affords recreation in growing city.

North of Phoenix

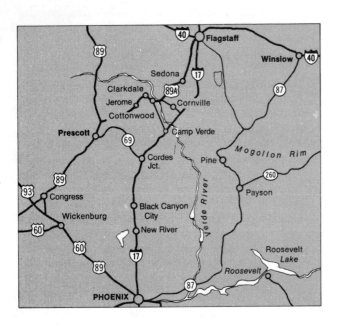

No visitor can claim to know Arizona without having visited the historic and varied country north of Phoenix. Here is where Arizona changes its face, the lowland desert rising to meet the 200-mile-long escarpment of the Mogollon Rim. Here cactus and Sonora shrubbery give way to junipers on rolling hills and thick pine forest near and above the rim. Cutting through this transition zone are wild and beautiful gorges carved by silt-loaded rivers, as well as sky-reaching buttes and pinnacles of colorful sandstone exposed by erosion. Throughout the area are the relics of prehistoric cliff-dwelling and pueblo-building Indians, the prospectors and miners who searched and dug for copper and gold, and the soldiers, pioneers, and cattle kings who settled and subdued the Wild West. You will find much to interest you north of Phoenix; plan to take time to explore it in leisurely fashion.

Three highways fan out northward from Phoenix. U.S. Highway 89-60 heads northwest to Wickenburg and its "sun country" and on to Kingman (where it meets Interstate Highway 40), the Colorado River, and northern Mohave County. From Wickenburg, U.S. 89 curves northeastward to Prescott, and U.S. 60 heads westward toward Quartzsite and Blythe, California (see Southwestern Arizona). The major highway from Phoenix is Interstate 17, the "Black Canyon Freeway," heading straight north toward Flagstaff, with connecting highways turning off to Prescott, the Verde Valley, and Sedona (see "Side Trips from Old Route 66"). A smaller highway, but often considered the most scenic of all three, is Arizona State Highway 87, the "Beeline Highway," going northeast from Scottsdale into the Tonto Basin and the most spectacular cliffs of the Mogollon Rim.

SUN COUNTRY

From November to May is the favored vacation time in the area around Wickenburg in Arizona's famed sun country, northwest of Phoenix. Wickenburg claims almost year-long sunshine. Records give it an average of 292 sunny days a year. Winters offer sun-soaked days and clear, crisp evenings, with temperatures ranging from 45° to 85°.

Out Wickenburg way

Wickenburg, with a population of about 3,000, lies along the Hassayampa River at an altitude of 2,093 feet. It's a town that still retains some of the flavor of the Old West. Its Frontier Street has buildings with false fronts, overhanging roofs, and hitching posts. The Desert Caballeros Western Museum features 30,000 square feet of displays depicting Wickenburg's glamorous history, from early Indian through modern Western artists.

The town was named for Henry Wickenburg, who, according to one legend, threw a rock at his burro in 1863. Since the rock was heavy with gold, it fell short of its mark. In this way, the Vulture Mine was discovered; during the two decades after its discovery, it turned out 30 million dollars in gold.

Wickenburg was once the gold capital of Arizona, but now its residents call it the dude ranch capital of the world. Some of the spreads

TINY, tranquil Granite Basin Lake is tucked away in forested country north of Prescott. The five-acre lake is stocked with warm-water game fish.

WIDE OPEN SPACES near Wickenburg are dude ranch country, where big spreads combine working ranches with resort facilities. Guided horseback rides are by far the most popular activity.

are big, working cattle ranches. Guests are encouraged to join such activities as roundups and branding. Guest ranches have frequent gymkhanas during their season. Contestants are the ranch guests, and the public is invited to watch.

Activities include swimming, tennis, trap shooting, golf, and—by far the most popular of all—horseback riding. The riding terrain is wide-open country: cholla-studded mesas; tawny, tumbled hills ornamented with the tall arms of the saguaro cactus; and the purple-colored mountains. There are guided breakfast rides, chuck wagon picnics along the lazing Hassayampa River, and overnight pack trips up rocky canyon trails.

Once a year, generally the second week in February, tourists from far and wide descend on Wickenburg for the rambunctious Gold Rush Days festivities. Official start of the three-day celebration comes when the Gold Shirt Gang captures the town on Friday and raises its outlaw flag over the city hall. From here on in, there is activity galore. Parades, dances,

rodeos, gold panning, a gem show, arts and crafts exhibits, a carnival, and melodramas fill the three days.

Accommodations in the Wickenburg area are many and varied. For information and brochures, write to the Roundup Club (Wickenburg's version of a Chamber of Commerce), P.O. Drawer CC, Wickenburg, AZ 85358.

The Roundup Club also makes available a "Stay-A-Day" packet of information on the points of interest and visitor activities in the area.

The Vulture Mine

About 14 miles southwest of Wickenburg is the Vulture Mine discovered by Henry Wickenburg. On a walking tour you'll see the old rock house with walls 3 feet thick, the big dining hall, the assay laboratory cluttered with dusty equipment, and workers' quarters. Other interesting features include a gallows-type frame over the old shaft, the jailhouse, and the nearby hanging tree. Walls of the older buildings are built of bricks made of local clay and tailings; fine particles of gold shine in the sun.

You reach the mine by following U.S. 60 westward for 2 miles out of Wickenburg, then heading south 12 miles on the well-marked Vulture Mine road. It's a well-kept gravel road but one that rises and descends over a succession of dips and low ridges until you get the impression you're on a gentle roller-coaster.

The mine is open daily with guided tours on weekends. There's a small admission fee.

The Joshua Forest

One of the best concentrations of Joshua trees *(Yucca brevifolia)* in the West is along the Joshua Tree Parkway on U.S. Highway 93. You enter the parkway 22 miles northwest of Wickenburg and continue for 16 miles through fine stands of Joshua trees protected in this state reserve. Beginning as early as the end of February and often lasting through the first weeks of April, the trees are in bloom, with large clusters of pale greenish white flowers at their branch tips. U.S. 93 is apt to be busy with traffic, but a sheltered roadside rest and numerous broad turnouts along the parkway invite you to stop and enjoy the blossom display.

A sampling of ghosts

From north of Wickenburg, U.S. 89 turns north 10 miles to the small settlement of Congress, then turns northeast to wind over the mountains into the Prescott National Forest and into the mid-forest city of Prescott.

Although Congress is not a true ghost town, there are some ruined slabs and foundations on a hill to the north. The present-day town is an active community along the road, with mobile homes and permanently-settled trailers augmenting permanent structures.

However, a dirt road turning south from the highway 2 miles northeast of Congress leads to sites of old mining developments and to one ghost town that is now coming to life again as gold draws prospectors and miners back into the hills.

It's 6 miles from the highway to the rocky canyon in which the settlement of Stanton is staging a comeback. The town grew up around the Antelope Station stage stop put there in 1875 and subsequently took the name of a promoter who developed some notoriety. Stanton grew to include a stamp mill (for gold production from ore mined in the adjacent Rich Hill) and at least a dozen houses, a store, and miner's

boardinghouse. By 1905, it had faded, and the post office was closed.

Around on the east side of Rich Hills, reached by another dirt road, is the site of the Octave mine, which was active from 1900 to 1942. Some stone walls and foundations mark the sites of the former buildings, and there are heaps of mine tailings. Rockhounds hunt here for pieces of iron pyrites ("fool's gold") found encased in chunks of white quartz; it's sometimes used for jewelry but is of little commercial value.

Avoid those dirt roads in rainy weather; stay out of abandoned mine shafts, for they could collapse.

Yarnell Hill Lookout

The Stanton-Octave side road climbs steeply out of the north end of the canyon to meet U.S. 89 at Yarnell. If you've made the canyon drive, it's worthwhile to turn left into the southbound lane (back toward Wickenburg) for less than a mile to the roadside lookout point on the west slope of Yarnell Hill. It probably takes in more of Arizona than any highway view stop in the state—a tremendous, sweeping view across the desert to distant mountains. You can see a rain or dust storm west of Wickenburg or watch lightning play through a summer thunderhead down toward Gila Bend. A low tower facilitates the view.

If you're driving up U.S. 89 from Congress Junction, the highway is divided here, and you'll have to go past the lookout about a half-mile before you can U-turn and come back on the south-bound lane.

PRESCOTT AND VICINITY

Prescott's site was chosen in 1864 by the men sent west by President Lincoln to organize a government for the new Territory of Arizona. Governor John Goodwin picked a spot at the edge of a vast pine forest that has a climate its residents ever since have considered close to ideal. The cycle of distinct seasons brings in turn the changing colors of fall, an occasional winter snowstorm, the gradual greening of spring, and then matchless summer days—temperatures in the 70s or 80s, blue morning skies with cotton-white clouds billowing up around noon, often an afternoon thunderstorm to freshen the air, then the long mountain twilight. And at night—except when the moon out-

COVERED WAGON carries out Frontier Days theme in parade held during Prescott's annual four-day Fourth of July celebration.

COOL PINE FOREST borders part of trail to Thumb Butte in Prescott National Forest. Elsewhere along the 1½-mile trail, cactus mingles with mountain vegetation.

glows them—more stars shine than you ever imagined existed.

From the beginning, Prescott has been a center of mining and cattle ranching. It appropriately claims to be the birthplace of the distinctively American sport of rodeo. The community traces its annual Frontier Days celebration from 1888, but there is evidence of an even earlier rodeo here—a silver buckle engraved, "Prescott July 4th, 1886, Best Time 59½ Sec."

Prescott has an 18-hole golf course (Antelope Hills Municipal), public tennis courts and swimming pools, and five nearby lakes popular with fishermen: Lynx, Willow, Watson, Granite Basin, and Goldwater.

Those interested in camping, hiking, or riding will find almost unlimited opportunity. East and north of Prescott the country opens into rolling, juniper-studded hills and the curious rock formations of the Granite Dells area, then settles into the sweeping, mountain-rimmed expanses of Lonesome and Chino valleys. In contrast, west and south of town are forested mountain ridges and basins covered with ponderosa pine and Douglas fir. This is part of Prescott National Forest, which contains 18 recreation developments, several within minutes of Prescott.

Here are some of the main places of interest in and near Prescott. For additional information on events, activities, facilities, and points of interest in the Prescott area, inquire at or write to the Chamber of Commerce, Box 1147, Prescott.

The Plaza. Dominating the broad walk on the north side of the Yavapai County Courthouse is a dynamic equestrian statue, a memorial to the Rough Riders. It portrays Captain William (Bucky) O'Neill, former Prescott mayor and sheriff who was killed in action in Cuba in 1898. The bronze sculpture is the work of Solon Borglum, brother of Gutzon Borglum of Mount Rushmore fame.

Of the business blocks that face the plaza, one is more famous than the rest: it is part of Montezuma Street, better known as Whiskey Row.

Opposite the southeast corner of the plaza is the modern city hall, featuring mural paintings by Paul Coze.

The Chamber of Commerce, a good source of information, is opposite the southwest corner of the big courthouse, on Goodwin Street, around the corner from U.S. 89 (Montezuma Street).

Sharlot Hall Museum. Three blocks west on Gurley Street, the stone Sharlot Hall museum building, filled with mementoes of pioneer days and displays of Indian art and crafts, shares a landscaped site with several structures typical of Prescott a century ago. The buildings include the first Governor's Mansion, containing period furniture, tools, photos, and relics of pioneer days; the first house in the town; a reconstruction of the first schoolhouse; Bashford House, an 1878 Victorian, two rooms of which provide gallery space for Prescott's Mountain Artists Guild; and the John C. Fremont House, furnished in period antiques. The complex is open weekdays except Monday and afternoons on Sundays. Admission is free.

Smoki Museum. Across town at Willis Street and Arizona Avenue, the Smoki people display a fine collection of Indian objects—prehistoric, historic, and contemporary. The museum is open from June 1 to September 1. Hours are 10 a.m. to 4:30 p.m. weekdays (closed Mondays), 1 to 5 p.m. Sunday. Admission is free.

The Smoki are a cross-section of Prescott business and professional people whose organization grew out of a lighthearted parody of an Indian snake dance at a community celebration in 1921. The incident started a group of Prescott men thinking about the mystery and beauty of many tribal rituals.

The society that resulted has now earnestly pursued for almost half a century that objec-

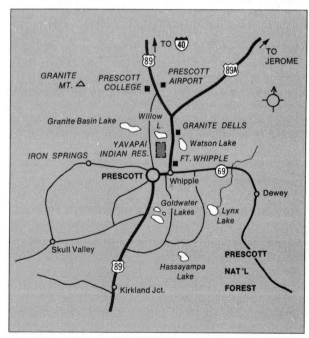

PRESCOTT vicinity enjoys seasonal changes and attracts rodeo riders, tourists, and sportsmen.

tive of studying and perpetuating the songs, legends, and ceremonies of American Indian tribes. Each year in August, the group presents a unique pageant of Indian songs and dances, culminating in the spectacular Smoki snake dance, based on the famous rain dance of the Hopis. Some Indians have resented the Smoki reenactment of their religious rituals; others, however, have cooperated and assisted, and so have anthropologists and archeologists.

Fort Whipple

Less than a mile east of town on U.S. 89 is one of Arizona's historic Army posts, now a Veterans Administration hospital. Fort Whipple, first located a few miles away, was established on this site in May, 1864. From 1869 to 1886, the final years of the Apache campaigns, it was headquarters for the Military Department of Arizona.

Since 1918 it has been a hospital for disabled veterans. You are welcome to drive or walk around the tree-shaded grounds. The handsome buildings include former barracks and officers' homes. There is an information desk in the main hospital building.

Granite Dells

Near the junction of U.S. 89 and 89A, about 5 miles north of Prescott, the Granite Dells area is a pleasant stopping place for the tourist and a picnic and recreation spot for local residents. The upthrust rocks create a maze of small hideaways and rim two small lakes planted with warm-water game fish. The size of the lakes may fluctuate with the seasons, since they are irrigation reservoirs. Off U.S. 89A, a dirt road leads to a tree-shaded creek and picnic spots. There's a camping area north of Willow Lake.

Camping in the pines

The evergreen forests ringing Granite Dells on three sides offer many outdoor recreation areas and retreats and excellent camping. Granite Basin Lake is a warm-water fishing lake 10 miles northwest of Prescott on a year-round dirt road off the Iron Springs road. Lynx Lake, 7 miles east of town on Walker Road off State 69, and Goldwater Lake, 4.5 miles from downtown on the Senator Highway, are stocked with bluegill, trout, and crappies. All have Forest Service improved campgrounds nearby, and you'll find

larger campgrounds among the pines off of U.S. 89 about 3 miles south of town.

Local events

In the Prescott area the local events have a Western flavor evoking scenes of the pioneer past from this background.

Horse shows and racing. Yavapai County Fair Horse Show and Prescott Quarter Horse Show are in September; other horse shows are held during spring, summer, and fall.

Prescott Downs. Horse racing, with parimutuel betting, draws crowds every weekend from Memorial Day through Labor Day, except during the Smoki Ceremonials and Frontier Days.

Frontier Days. This is the big Fourth of July celebration, with four days of parades, fireworks, and the original rodeo.

Ranch Tours. The Chamber of Commerce and Yavapai Cattlegrowers co-sponsor tours of working ranches every Tuesday for six summer weeks. Drive your own car in caravan. Ask the Chamber for the schedule.

PRESCOTT TO FLAGSTAFF

Several miles north of Prescott, U.S. 89 swings north through cattle country and juniper forests to meet U.S. 66 at Ash Fork. It passes through the farming settlement of Chino Valley and, about 4.5 miles beyond, past the Del Rio Ruins, moundlike remnants located between the highway and the railroad.

U.S. 89A, a more scenic route, branches northeast, connecting with U.S. 66 at Flagstaff. The highway climbs above 7,000 feet at Mingus Mountain and drops down into the Verde Valley. For details of this route see pages 33-36.

NORTH ON INTERSTATE 17

The most direct and heavily traveled route from Phoenix to Flagstaff is Interstate 17, the "Black Canyon Highway," a divided freeway for most of its length.

Rising from the desert floor to the pine-clad Mogollon Plateau, the highway takes you through the transition between two faces of Arizona: the dry, blazing Sonora desert and the green, heavily-forested highlands where winter snow lies deep.

Along the route you pass historic sites and turnoffs into beautiful and primitive back country. For details of the area north of Cordes Junction see pages 33-36.

Phoenix to New River

North of Phoenix are intersecting roads connecting to Scottsdale, Carefree, and Cave Creek on the east and to U.S. 89-60 on the west at Surprise. About 20 miles north of the city, a turnoff westward takes you to the authentically reconstructed settlement of Pioneer Arizona (see page 60) and to the Lake Pleasant recreation area. About 6 miles beyond, at New River, a gravel road reaches back southeast to Cave Creek.

Agua Fria Canyon

Single day hikes or longer back-packing trips are enjoyable in this 13-mile-long canyon, undisturbed by roads, along the Agua Fria River. The upper end is the most interesting; here the ruins of the 70-year-old Richinbar Mine buildings sprawl on a hillside, with its hanging flume strung along the canyon. You can hike in 3 miles to the mine from the upper end of the canyon or go all the way down to where the canyon nears the highway. To reach the top, turn east off Interstate 17 at the Badger Springs exit 3 miles north of Sunset Point and follow the right fork of the road to Badger Creek, from where you hike down to the river. To reach the bottom end of the canyon, take the Squaw Valley exit near Black Canyon City, follow the Squaw Valley Road east for ¼ mile, turn left on the Riverbend Road and left again at the fork, and go 2 miles to the canyon.

Bumble Bee

About 3 miles north of Black Canyon City, a side road turns off eastward and then branches. Take the north fork (it's marked) and follow 5 miles of seasonal dirt road to Bumble Bee.

This same dirt road was the main road from Phoenix to Flagstaff until 1955, when State 79, now the freeway, was built. The old store building at Bumble Bee was first a Wells Fargo stage stop, then a Greyhound bus stop. Bumble Bee was never a mining center, and it's not a "ghost town," even though prospectors bought supplies here. Behind the store is a "city street" lined with old buildings gathered

up in the vicinity and reassembled here. It's picturesque and, though artificial, typical of the real thing.

Horsethief Basin

Nestled high in the mountains of Prescott National Forest east of Bumble Bee, Horsethief Basin is a cool retreat from summer heat. In this fully-developed recreation area 6,000 feet high in the Bradshaw Mountains, pine and chaparral-covered slopes attract picnickers and campers from April to October. You can follow hiking trails and hook panfish in the small lake. When the ranger is on duty, you can visit the lookout tower for a panoramic view.

The Forest Service maintains improved campgrounds, including some enclosed wooden sleeping shelters as well as tent and trailer spaces. The concession-operated Horsethief Basin Resort (4723 North 40th Avenue, Phoenix, 85019) offers housekeeping cabins and a small store.

To reach Horsethief Basin from Interstate 17, take the Bumble Bee turnoff. About 5 miles north of Bumble Bee, take the left fork (it's marked) about 16 miles to the old mining town of Crown King, another 7 miles to the basin.

Sunset Point

The Sunset Point rest area, about 3 miles north of Bumble Bee turnoff, is the type of roadside pulloff you'd like to find along all major highways. In 1972 it won first prize among 70 entries from 28 states in a Federal Highway Administration competition. Four large ramadas on the hill west of the highway each shade seven picnic tables, and each table shares the same broad view over the valley to the Bradshaw Mountains. A central ramada contains restrooms, water, and map and photo displays of regional points of interest. From an overlook 100 feet below, you have an unobstructed view, including the old stage road, the cluster of buildings at Bumble Bee, and a portion of Horsethief Basin.

East of Interstate 17

From New River north to Cordes Junction, the highway is paralleled on the east at about 5 miles distance by the western borders of first the Tonto, then the Coconino national forests. Few roads penetrate the area, but one gravel road makes a long sweep back south. The

Bloody Basin road turns off east about 3 miles south of Cordes Junction and turns south to the Seven Springs and Horseshoe recreation areas. You'll find Forest Service campgrounds, with trailer space, at Seven Springs and on upper Cave Creek and at Horseshoe and Bartlett Lake, 15 miles west of the road on the Verde River. It's 39 miles along this back-road route south to Carefree and Scottsdale Boulevard. Ask about road conditions first, particularly during the rainy season.

MOGOLLON RIM COUNTRY

For more than 200 miles, the escarpment of the Mogollon Rim angles across the Arizona uplands, marking the edge of the high plateau and tracing a magnificent stretch of scenic vacation land. In a land where dramatic terrain is commonplace, it is remarkable for its jutting height and bold cliffs, but most of all for its length.

Seen from the air, the rim (its name is pronounced *Mo*-gee-own or *Mug*-ee-own) can be traced from the juniper-dotted hills near Ash Fork to the Blue Range of eastern Arizona before it finally disappears into the Mogollon Mountains of New Mexico. Here and there it has been obscured by encroaching canyons and jumbled mountains, but over most of its length it is distinct, a wall of rock sometimes white, sometimes blue-gray or red or cream. Reaching away in the distance, it is the most abrupt feature of the rugged zone that separates the plateau country from the desert to the south.

In shaping this wall, the forces of erosion have bared great layers of limestone, sandstone, and shale and bitten deep into the underlying granite. Like the rocks of the Grand Canyon, some of the sedimentary layers were laid down beneath the ocean; their presence today more than a mile above sea level is evidence that, some time in the geologic past, the whole area was uplifted out of the sea.

Along the line of the rim, above its cliffs and down in its shadow, stretches a quiet forest that beckons the hiker and rider and camper, the angler and hunter, and the auto explorer. Above the rim, aspen gleams against the dark green of Ponderosa pine and Douglas fir; below are broad stands of pine before the land slopes away toward the desert, where bare buttes and stark peaks shape the southern horizon. In fall, bright splotches of color reveal the presence of maple and oak above the rim and in the heads of the canyons at the rim's foot.

Toward the west end of the rim country is the Oak Creek Canyon area (see page 33), reached by U.S. 89A. Far to the east, two other principal highways slice through the rim: U.S. 60-State 77, linking central Arizona with U.S. 66; and U.S. 666, the winding, scenic Coronado Trail (see page 83).

The heart of the rim country lies between Highways 87 and 60, along that portion called locally the Tonto Rim, from Strawberry across Punkin Center and Pleasant Valley and eastward into the reservation of the White Mountain Apaches.

Details concerning accommodations, rental of horses, pack trips, and other facilities and services in the rim country can be obtained by writing to the Payson Chamber of Commerce, Drawer A, Payson, AZ 85541.

Historic ground

Tonto Basin, ancestral hunting ground of several Apache groups, was the scene of frequent Indian raids and of skirmishes between Apaches and soldiers from the nearest army posts—Camp Verde to the west, Camp (later Fort) Apache to the east, Fort McDowell to the south.

When these battles were over (the last one was fought in this area), trouble arose among the settlers themselves. Some of the West's bloodiest feuds between sheepmen and cattlemen were fought in the Pleasant Valley War from 1887 to 1892. Many spots in the vicinity of Young are remembered as scenes of ambushes and gun fights during the prolonged series of skirmishes.

Young is still on a graded dirt road running north and south between State 260 east of Christopher Creek and the east end of Roosevelt Lake. Inquire locally about road conditions in wet weather.

Zane Grey's cabin

The rim country has become familiar to thousands of readers of Zane Grey's western novels. *To the Last Man* is based on the Pleasant Valley War, and several of his other books, including *Under the Tonto Rim*, are set in this area.

The author lived for several years in a house just under the rim near the headwaters of Tonto Creek. The house has been restored and is maintained and opened to the public by a resident caretaker. Exhibits include copies of some of the original manuscripts and some first editions. The most important thing about

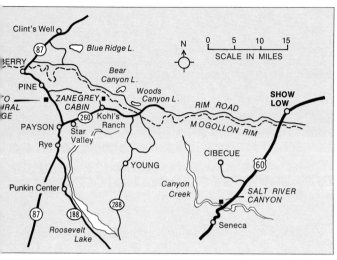

MOGOLLON Rim country features spectacular scenery, was the setting for Zane Grey novels.

the house is the setting: the rim looming behind and distant views over the tumbled pine forests of the basin below.

To reach the road to the cabin (and to the Tonto Creek trout hatchery), turn off State 260 just west of Kohl's Ranch resort and follow the gravel road up Tonto Creek. Inquire first at Kohl's Ranch for road conditions.

Along boulder-strewn Tonto Creek are picnic sites and a campground. It's a popular fishing and recreation area.

Viewing the rim

State 260 from Payson east climbs up the rim east of Christopher Creek. Along the road you can have close-up views of the weathered sandstone layers on one hand and panoramic views over the Tonto Basin on the other. It's one of the most scenic drives you'll find.

For longer views of the rambling escarpment from below, drive the control road between Kohl's Ranch resort and State 87 just below Pine. You'll go through dense forest, cross the East Verde River, and through gaps in the pines you'll see the massive wall of rock rearing to the north.

More good views of the massive rim come into sight in the vicinity of Pine and Strawberry on State 87.

The rim road, which runs along the top of the escarpment all the way from Camp Verde on Interstate 17 into the White Mountains east of U.S. 60, is also a great view drive, but it's a seasonal road. Ask about road conditions before setting out.

Tonto Natural Bridge

The Pine road that goes northwest from Payson offers a pleasant drive that takes you to Tonto Natural Bridge. The turnoff to the bridge is 12 miles from Payson. A 3-mile graded road leads to a guest lodge; the parking lot above the bridge is ¼ mile farther. You approach on a level with the top of the bridge, so you are unaware of the remarkable formation until you reach a proper vantage point to look down into the canyon of Pine Creek. Arching 183 feet above the creek, the great travertine span shades a cool, rocky vault below. Piles of boulders have dammed the creek to form a quiet pool. You'll find picnic tables under scattered shade trees. A short, steep trail takes you down under the bridge. Tonto Bridge is privately owned, and there's a small admission charge.

Hunting and fishing

The rim country probably has a wider variety of wild game than any other area in the state. Deer (both whitetail and mule), elk, javelina, black bear, and turkey are all found here, as well as many smaller kinds of game animals.

The big brown and rainbow trout probably draw more people to the rim country than any other single attraction. There are at least two dozen well-stocked trout streams in the area and several beautiful lakes, including a string of six artificial lakes in the Sitgreaves and Coconino national forests, excavated and stocked by the Arizona Game and Fish Department.

Blue Ridge Reservoir, 6 miles east of Clint's Well, off Arizona 87 north of the rim, offers more than 70 acres of fishing water planted with brown and rainbow trout. Farther east and close to the drop-off are the smaller Knoll, Bear Canyon, Woods Canyon, and Willow Spring Lakes reached by the rim road west of Arizona 260. East of that highway about 5 miles, on another dirt road, is Black Canyon Lake.

Camping in rim country

Forest Service improved campgrounds are situated near all the six lakes, along with one at the Canyon Point overlook off Arizona 260 just above the rim, one at Christopher Creek below the rim off the same highway, one at Ponderosa 14 miles east of Payson, one 5 miles north of Payson at the East Verde crossing of Arizona 87, one just outside Strawberry, and one more at Kehl Springs on the rim northeast of Strawberry, 7 miles east of Arizona 87 on a dirt road.

East of Phoenix

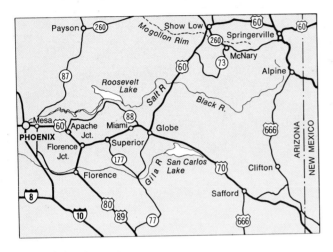

Between Phoenix and the New Mexico border stretches a fascinating land, offering travel surprises to the highway driver as well as to the side road explorer.

Within it are big lakes, spectacular scenic routes, two Apache Indian reservations, part of the Mogollon Rim, the dramatic Salt River Canyon, and the high pine forests and trout waters of the beautiful White Mountains.

East and northeast of Phoenix lies the Tonto National Forest, one of the largest national forests in the nation. Much of the "forest" is actually rolling desert, densely covered with creosote bush, palo verde, ironwood, and cactus of many varieties, including magnificent stands of saguaro. Winter rains make the desert blossom in the spring.

Near Phoenix, a series of dams interrupts the flow of the Salt River to make a 60-mile-long chain of lakes—the reservoirs that turned the lower Salt River Valley into rich citrus and cotton land, beginning in the early 1900s. Besides irrigation water and power, they provide recreation: camping, swimming, water skiing, motor boating, sailing, and fishing for warm-water fish. All four lakes—Saguaro, Canyon, Apache, and Roosevelt—have Forest Service picnic areas, a few campgrounds, rustic resorts, boats for rent, tackle, and bait.

The dramatic Apache Trail road paralleling the Salt River lakes is one of the state's most famous scenic drives; the major highway that swings south around the Superstition Wilderness presents quite different rocky landscapes. Together, they're a good day's loop trip from either Phoenix or Globe.

Alongside U.S. Highway 70 lies another man-made lake, San Carlos Reservoir. Farther to the southeast are the green fields of the upper Gila Valley.

The motorist following U.S. 60 to the border passes from desert to pines. He winds through magnificent gorges and rolls across plateaus. Side roads lead to desert lakes and reservoirs, to mountain lakes and streams, to cool forests. Before the highway reaches New Mexico, it ascends to nearly 7,000 feet and runs through deep snow in some winters.

Just south of State 260 is Arizona's newest winter sports complex, the Sunrise Ski Area developed by the Whiteriver Apaches.

Between the two major highways, close to the Arizona-New Mexico border the beautiful Coronado Trail winds through the White Mountain summer and autumn recreation areas.

PHOENIX TO GLOBE

The route from Phoenix to Globe forks at Apache Junction, in front of the imposing battlements of the Superstition Mountains; you can choose between the scenic Apache Trail or the more direct U.S. 60.

The left fork, the spectacular Apache Trail, leads to Roosevelt, Canyon, Apache lakes, and the north side of the Superstition Wilderness. It includes 25 miles of gravel road and is not a through route for trailers or big vans. Smaller trailers can manage the lake campground roads, but the real obstacle for larger vehicles is a series of sharp turns around the cliffs just below Roosevelt Dam.

The south fork is the major highway (U.S. 60) through Superior and Miami. En route are the Superstition Film Studios movie set, the turnoff to the north end of the Pinal Pioneer Parkway to Tucson, rocky Queen Creek Canyon, the Boyce Thompson Southwestern Arboretum, and the eroded sandstone pillars of Devil's Canyon.

(Continued on page 74)

*THE APACHE TRAIL, colorful with wildflowers in spring, zigzags along the 60-mile chain
of lakes formed by dams along the Salt River. View above is a few curves below Roosevelt Dam.*

*IN A BURST OF GLORY, poppies blanket
the hills in Tonto National Monument.*

Although most travelers start a Phoenix-Globe loop tour from Phoenix, starting from Globe will put the sun behind you in the morning going west and again in the evening heading east, a definite advantage. Either way, if you drive this loop as a one-day trip, take the Apache Trail first; explore a canyon, take a cooling splash in a lake, enjoy the scenery, and study the Tonto ruins. You will probably take longer than you expected; the southern route is easier and faster for a return drive.

The Apache Trail

This ancient Indian short-cut through the mountains is now Arizona State Highway 88, a dramatic, scenic drive through a wild region of tumbled volcanic debris and massive layered buttes, twisting tortuously through cliff-sided canyons and skirting sparkling lakes.

Starting at Apache Junction just west of the starkly eroded dacite cones of the Superstition Mountains, the road turns northeast into the foothills.

Goldfield to Tortilla Flat. A roadside curio shop marks the site of the ghost town of Goldfield. Next to the shop is a patched adobe building, once the mining camp's schoolhouse, now a snack bar and the only surviving building. Across the road you'll find the bones of the old town: crumbling foundations and debris from tumbled buildings. Behind the shop, the open shaft of the Bluebird Mine now displays minerals and relics of mining days.

About a mile beyond the mine, at a vista point, a gravel road turns west to First Water Creek and hiking trails into the Superstition Wilderness Area. Penetrating this rugged wilderness on foot or on horseback can be a challenging adventure in spring or fall. It's cold in winter. In summer, lack of water and extreme heat create hazardous conditions.

You must carry all the water you will need since the few permanent waterholes are difficult to find. U.S. Geological Survey maps are recommended equipment for this area. For pack-trip information and lists of packers, go to the Apache Junction Chamber of Commerce.

The road to Canyon Lake descends through eroded, folded lava flows to picnic areas and one campground and boat launching facilities.

East of Canyon Lake, the road swings south, separated from the chain of lakes by intervening buttes and mesas. There's a store, restaurant, motel, and gas pump at Tortilla Flat, east of the lake (19 miles from Apache Junction). It's

29 miles on this road to the next store at Roosevelt Lake, or you can take a steep side road to the Apache Lake Resort about 16 miles east.

Fish Creek Canyon. East of Tortilla Flat the switchbacks climb through rock-walled canyons. The walls are a natural museum of rock formations: pink layers of arkose rock cut by dikes of tan lava dusted with glittering specks of quartz and feldspar.

Five miles east of Tortilla Flat, just beyond another vista point, the paved road ends, and the gravel road continues through the most dramatic part of the drive to Roosevelt Lake.

The sharp, winding road descends down the cliffs into Fish Creek Canyon and takes you to the one-lane bridge across the creek. The narrow fissure of the canyon opens south to views of sunlit Geronimo Head. It's a good spot for a pause, a picnic in the stream-bed oasis, or a short exploratory hike. The terrain is rough; proceed cautiously. An inviting shallow cave is accessible in the west wall of the canyon.

Apache Lake. From the Apache Trail a gravel road descends sharply to the Apache Lake resort and marina—motel, store, restaurant, boating and fishing supplies. From this saguaro-lined road you can view the Painted Cliffs and Goat Mountain across the lake. Tonto National Forest Service picnic grounds and campsites are near the lake. A turnoff farther east on the Apache Trail takes you to the campgrounds of Burnt Corral.

Roosevelt Lake. Roosevelt Dam, wedged into a deep canyon, is the world's largest masonry dam. It was the first project under the Reclamation Act, begun in 1905, completed in 1911 and dedicated by Teddy Roosevelt himself. Viewed downstream, where the gravelled Apache Trail loops tightly around almost vertical ridges, it resembles a smaller Hoover Dam. Behind it, the largest of the interior Arizona reservoirs spreads broadly east and north against the Sierra Ancha Range and the Zane Grey Hills.

The lake is a popular boating, water-skiing, and fishing site, and there are several Forest Service minimum facility campsites. State 88 from the dam to Globe is paved. A store and gas station are located about 2 miles southeast of the dam. Motel, restaurant, and gas station are located at Roosevelt Lake Resort about 6 miles southeast of the dam.

Four Peaks. North of Apache Lake, you reach the Four Peaks area of the southern Mazatzal

Mountains by a jeep road from State 188. This remote area offers summit views of the Tonto Basin to the northeast and the Salt River Valley southwest. There's a primitive camp area at Pigeon Spring, 10 miles southwest of State 188 on the El Oso Road. If the road's in good shape, you can drive all the way to the camp.

At the Pigeon Spring camping area you will find plenty of firewood, but you must bring your own drinking water. Here the trail drops from 5,600 feet to 3,800 feet at Big Oak Flat, where a gravel road winds back to State 188.

Other trails throughout the Mazatzal Mountains are marked on U.S. Geological Survey quadrangle sheets and Forest Service trail maps. You can obtain these and more details at Mesa or Roosevelt ranger stations or at the Forest Service headquarters in Phoenix.

Tonto National Monument. Cliff dwellings—occupied more than 600 years ago by the Salado Indians, who irrigated and farmed the Salt River Valley—are preserved in this canyon about 3 miles southeast of Roosevelt Dam.

At the visitors' center you can inspect their tools, weapons, jewelry, pottery, and fine weaving. Dioramas depict the community as reconstructed from archeological studies.

A half-hour's walk (through a show of wildflowers in April) will take you to the Lower Ruin where you can wander through its 19 rooms. A visit to the more distant, 40-room Upper Ruin must be arranged at least four days in advance. The Lower Ruin is tucked into a cave and is in deep shade by mid-afternoon.

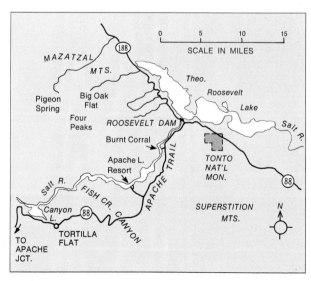

TWISTING, scenic Apache Trail takes a dramatic route through cliff-sided canyons.

The southern route

The wide, divided highway on this route to Globe is a stark contrast to the rugged curves of the Apache Trail. East of Apache Junction, U.S. 60 affords spectacular views of the legendary Superstition Mountains. About 7 miles west of the junction, a 2½-mile side road leads to Superstition, a permanent television and movie set at the base of the mountains. This detailed replica of a 19th-century western town comprises about two dozen clapboard and adobe buildings ranged along intersecting streets.

At Florence Junction, U.S. 80-89 turns south to the scenic back road to Tucson.

A Desert Arboretum. Established and maintained as a research institution, this Desert Biology Station of the University of Arizona, near Superior, has become a popular rest stop and tour attraction. The remarkable collection of plant, animal, and bird life makes a visit a fascinating experience. Here you can see 6,000 botanical species from around the world and more than 150 kinds of birds and 40 species of animals.

Marked nature trails take you through the exhibits. One—about an hour's walk—includes the cottonwood-cooled canyon of Queen Creek. There's also a shaded picnic area.

Looming behind the Boyce Thompson Southwestern Arboretum, the 4,400-foot Picket Post Mountain marks the site of an army heliograph communication station used for signaling during the Apache Wars.

Superior. At the edge of town visitors can see the entrance to the 3,500-foot shaft and the adjacent smelter of one of the few underground copper mines in Arizona. A steep slope topped by a sheer, vertically eroded rock wall known as Apache Leap rims the town on the east. The name originated in a story of Indian warriors who flung themselves from the rock's top to escape capture by soldiers.

Just west of Superior, a sign marks a dirt sideroad leading to Apache Tears Cave, where you can find the small, gem-like obsidian accretions called Apache Tears embedded in layers of perlite, a mineral mined for use in insulation. The one-mile drive to the cave is a rough road and, after a rain, requires 4-wheel-drive traction.

DESERT RUINS left by the Salado Indians are preserved in Tonto National Monument (page 75). In the Lower Ruins shown at right, you can wander through 19 rooms of the ancient cliff dwellings.

The Globe area

Long hills of mine tailings and slag are scattered between Miami and Globe. The light-colored rubble is waste from the crusher, called tailings. The dark red to black material is burned rock from the smelter, called slag.

Once a rip-snorting copper mining town, the thriving trade center and travelers' stopover of Globe still shows many traces of its frontier beginnings. Downtown, the ornate false fronts of the early 1900s mingle with modern business facades. On a hill above the city stand the ruins of the played-out mine that once sustained the booming town.

The Globe of today is still a busy place: center for mining supplies, county seat of Gila County, gateway to a cattle empire to the east, and a popular residential city for those who like or need its climate, halfway between desert and mountain.

Miami is a good place to go if you want to understand the copper recovery process. There's a free tour on weekdays of the Inspiration Consolidated Copper Company mine and smelter. The tour starts at 12:45 p.m. September through May, 9 a.m. June through August. It includes the open pit, the leaching plant, mill and concentrator, and the smelter; sign up at the company's employment office on U.S. 60.

South of Globe, Pinal Mountain Road takes you to the Salado Indian ruins and the campgrounds and trails of Pinal Peak.

Besh-Ba-Gowah. Although not as well preserved as the Tonto National Monument ruins left by the ancient Salado Indians, the Salado site at Besh-Ba-Gowah (meaning "metal camp") is considerably more extensive. Situated about a mile south of Globe on Pinal Mountain Road, the ruins cover about 2 acres on a bluff above Pinal Creek. During its active period, from about 1225 until 1400 A.D., this pueblo contained approximately 200 rooms. A sizable area of cultivated land surrounded the buildings. Now some two dozen roofless rooms are clearly defined by stone walls. You're free to roam the site at will, but do not remove anything. A small collection of artifacts from the ruins is on display in the Clara T. Woody Museum (open Monday through Saturday).

Pinal Peak. The highest and coolest campgrounds (about 7,800 feet) in the Tonto National Forest, and some scenic hiking trails, are atop timber-clad Pinal Peak, on a sometimes rough gravel road about 15 miles south of Globe.

If you'd like an easy hike and can find a driver to take you to the peak, you can enjoy the broad views of the Gila Valley on the way down the Sixshooter Trail. It's about a 2½-hour descent to where the trail comes out on Kellner Road; the driver should allow about a half hour to meet you at the bottom.

The campgrounds usually are open from May to December; exact dates depend on the weather. Check at the Forest Service office in Globe.

To drive to the peak, take Pinal Mountain Road (Forest Road 55), an extension of the Icehouse Canyon Road south out of Globe. Large trailers should not attempt the road.

APACHE COUNTRY

Traveling the main highways of east-central Arizona, you can't go far without entering the homeland of the state's Apache Indians. East of Globe, U.S. 70 crosses miles of the San Carlos Indian Reservation; here is big San Carlos Lake, a major fishing and water sports site. Winding through the mountains from Globe to Show Low and across the pine-forested plateau to Springerville, you drive through the Fort Apache Indian Reservation. The town of McNary and the western half of the beautiful White Mountain Recreation Area are on this reservation.

The two reservations, separated by the Black River, cover millions of acres of fine grazing range, farmlands, and forests. Both tribes encourage outdoor recreation on their reservations. The Whiteriver Apaches have the lakes and streams of the White Mountains and a ski area. Around one of the biggest lakes in Arizona, the San Carlos Apaches are developing thousands of acres of land for public recreational use. Year-round fishing is popular on both reservations—including ice fishing in the White Mountain lakes. The Fort Apache Reservation offers more numerous and varied waters but nothing as big as San Carlos Lake. Both tribes require a fishing permit in addition to an Arizona fishing license.

Hunting on both reservations is subject to state game laws, and tribes also impose their own fees and limits to conserve game species as valuable natural resources. Big game hunting is a major attraction. You can obtain permits for reservation hunting and fishing at sporting goods stores throughout the area.

Except for the principal highways, roads on the reservations are unsurfaced. Be sure to make local inquiries about travel conditions, especially during the summer rainy season (cloudbursts are common in July and August) or winter (when you'll likely find snow and ice in the highlands). It is always advisable to carry tire chains, shovel, and drinking water.

Visitors to the reservation capitals of both San Carlos and Whiteriver will find a tribal office to provide them with information about reservation points of interest. If you wish, staff members will explain the tribal enterprises—from cattle herds to retail shops.

Remember that, while on Indian land, you are subject to reservation laws. Fire control laws are enforced, and you will be expected to use great care with campfires, matches, and cigarettes. Finally, don't forget that courtesy requires you to ask permission before taking pictures of Indians or their homes.

San Carlos Reservation

You enter the reservation just east of Globe, where a turnoff at Peridot leads you to the reservation capital of San Carlos. Peridot is the name of a gem stone, olivine, frequently found in volcanic areas. The San Carlos Reservation is a major source. Hunting for them here, however, is not permitted. The tribe has strict mineral regulations.

The road to San Carlos follows the river through fields and big tamarisk trees. The town clusters around the low buildings of the Indian agency and the tribal council; the absence of garish signs and neon gives it the look of another era. If you need information, ask for it at the tribal office.

The San Carlos Apaches hold their annual celebration and rodeo during October on the three-day Veterans Day weekend. The traditional Sunrise Dance, performed during the weekend, honors Apache maidens' "coming out" and is highlighted by the colorful Crown Dancers, also known by the Apaches as the "Mountain Spirit Dancers." These dances are also performed at other times throughout the year, but the dates are not publicized. Although visitors are welcome and may take photographs, they should ask permission and keep in mind that the dances are serious religious ceremonies.

For detailed information about the reservation, write the San Carlos Tribe, San Carlos, AZ 85550.

Reservation lakes. The reservation encourages recreation at all three lakes by offering complete facilities for campers, boaters, and fishermen. Passenger cars can reach San Carlos and Seneca Lake year round. The road to Point of Pines Lake, like most other reservation roads, is best traveled by pickups and hardier vehicles, especially in winter and the July rainy season. Ask about conditions when taking off on a back road and watch for grazing stock.

San Carlos Lake. One of the Southwest's major reclamation structures, Coolidge Dam was completed in 1930 to provide irrigation water

THE LOST DUTCHMAN

Somewhere in the Superstition Mountains lies the answer to one of the most tantalizing mysteries of the Southwest—the legendary Lost Dutchman gold mine.

The mine takes its name from one of the few people who claimed to have found it and lived to tell about it. That was the "Dutchman," Jakob Walz, the solitary, immigrant prospector who periodically showed up with bags of nuggets to spend in Phoenix saloons, where he bragged about his fabulous strike but never revealed its whereabouts. If you believe the stories, he wasn't the first discoverer—nor the last.

Reportedly, the mine is somewhere near Weaver's Needle, the distinctive rock spire that is the most recognizable landmark along the Apache Trail. According to legends, the Indians called this area the home of the thunder gods (even today, thunderstorms breed in the broiling peaks to rumble and crackle over the countryside). They knew about the mine; it was a sacred place. Today, the Indian legend is overlaid with a new folklore: tales of old-timers, fragmentary reports, rumors, books, exhaustive research, and a motion picture starring Glenn Ford.

Despite the stories of treasure-seekers who never return and even the discovery of bullet-pierced skulls, thousands of treasure-hunters—from greenhorn tourists to experienced prospectors—have ventured into the Superstition Wilderness to look for the mine. Some are unaccounted for; others report hearing shots from nearby rocks. But if the Lost Dutchman exists, it is still keeping its secret.

and electricity for the upper Gila Valley. Its reservoir, San Carlos Lake, covers one of the ancient burial grounds of the Apaches. The Indians turned down a government offer to move the graves, considering this a desecration of the dead; the compromise was a great concrete slab on the lake floor that protects the graves from the waters above. A paved road follows the south shore of the reservoir for about 25 miles, rejoining the main highway near Bylas.

The Apaches call San Carlos Lake the hottest bass lake in the state. It's open for fishing all year. A reservation fishing permit is required. The lake is also a popular site for water-skiing, swimming, skindiving, boating, and waterfowl hunting, but check ahead—these activities are sometimes curtailed when water level is low.

Facilities at the San Carlos Marina Resort, at the west end of the lake, include a coffee shop, curio and tackle shop, and a camper-trailer park. This is the only lake on the reservation where gasoline motors are permitted; you can rent motor boats here.

Seneca Lake. Situated on U.S. 60 just south of the Salt River, this major development includes a restaurant, store, and picnic and campsites. The resort is open year round and in winter for ice fishing.

Point of Pines Lake. In the eastern part of the reservation, this year-round trout fishing site is difficult to reach after a rain without a four-wheel-drive vehicle.

To reach the lake and its campgrounds, turn north from U.S. 70 on the paved road 3 miles east of Peridot (Indian Service Route 8). After the pavement ends at Juniper, there's another 35 miles of dirt road eastward over the Nantac Pass and north to the lake.

Just off the road near the Route 11 intersection are the Arsenic Caves, where you will see ancient drawings on the cave walls and have a panoramic view of the reservation.

The Salt River Canyon

At the Salt River border between the two reservations, you descend into a small-scale Grand Canyon. Here U.S. 60 drops more than 2,000 feet over a series of wide switchbacks, then crosses a bridge and climbs back out.

On the south side (approaching from Globe), you'll find frequent overlooks and convenient picnic ramadas with tables a short walk off the highway. Concrete steps near the bridge lead down to a large picnic area. There's a small restaurant near the bridge.

About a half-mile upstream from the bridge, the Salt River tumbles over wide falls where an attractive picnic site is easily overlooked if you keep to the highway. To reach the falls and get a view from the bottom of the canyon, turn off the highway immediately north of the bridge and follow the narrow road upstream beside the river. Currents at the base of the falls make swimming dangerous here.

West of the highway bridge (about 7 miles downstream by dirt road on the north bank) are the eroded salt banks and shallow caves that probably gave the river its Spanish Colonial name, Rio Salado. You'll find campsites at the Cibecue Creek confluence—by the salt banks and west of them.

Catfish glide in the river. To fish for them you'll need, in addition to a valid Arizona fishing license, a special permit for the Fort Apache Indian Reservation. Permits are available at the store near the bridge.

Fort Apache Reservation

Until recently, most of the 1½ million acres of this reservation were accessible only by unpaved trail. Now, with the organization of the White Mountain Recreation Enterprise, the tribe has built access roads, campgrounds, lodging, and other facilities for visitors.

For detailed information, maps, and arrangements for groups, write to the White Mountain Recreation Enterprise, P.O. Box 218, Whiteriver, AZ 85941, or phone (602) 338-4385. Fishing, hunting, and camping permits may be obtained in advance from the same office or in person at sporting goods stores in Phoenix, Tucson, and towns throughout east-central Arizona.

A visit to the primitive settlement of Cibecue, any of the Indian trading posts, and tribal gatherings at which visitors are welcome will introduce you to the Apache people and their way of life.

The town of Show Low (see page 82) is a good point of departure for your visit to Whiteriver and the Fort Apache Reservation. Take State 260 southeast from Show Low; the turn-off on State 73 is at Indian Pine, between Pinetop and McNary. On the corner is the tribe's handsome, modern-rustic Hon-Dah motel and cabin complex. Hon-Dah means, "Welcome; come in; be our guest."

The highway descends gradually through pine forests and grassy meadows, past occasional corrals and loading chutes and grazing cattle, into open scrub juniper. Scattered among the vegetation are outcroppings and fragments of the coarse, dark volcanic rock called malapai, riddled with large holes like those bored by clams in ocean sandstone.

Whiteriver. Whiteriver is like many other small Southwestern towns—motel, gas stations, stores, small frame houses, and big trees, tribal offices and council chamber, a memorial hall, a municipal center, a Department of H.E.W. hospital, and housing developments. The difference here is that the people are the Apaches—among the last of the frontier tribes to accept the authority of the United States.

Here at Whiteriver is the studio, shop, and home of Jack Fowler, whose copper and brass sculptures of Western scenes are displayed in collections around the nation, including one at the White House. (In Phoenix, you'll see his 18-foot-tall "Sun Worshipper" near the intersection of 16th Street and Indian School Road.)

The Whiteriver Apaches hold their annual Tribal Fair and Rodeo in early August. Like their San Carlos neighbors, they conduct the Sunrise Maiden ceremonies.

Fort Apache. Three miles south of Whiteriver is historic Fort Apache, established in 1870, once a major army post and important in the Apache wars. It was from here that the U.S. Cavalry and the famous Apache Scouts went out after the marauding bands of Geronimo and Natchez.

In 1924 the fort was turned over to the Bureau of Indian Affairs and became the Theodore Roosevelt Indian School. Many of the original buildings still stand, identified by signs. Visitors are welcome.

Kinishba. Seven miles west of Fort Apache are the partially restored remains of Kinishba ("red house" in Apache), a pueblo-type village of the classic Pueblo-III period, which housed up to 2,000 people near the end of the 13th century.

The two large buildings, and several smaller outlying structures, have more than 400 rooms. A major archeological discovery, Kinishba has been an important training and field research center for the University of Arizona.

From Kinishba it is about 24 miles northwest through a colorful land of red mountains and dark green junipers to a junction with U.S. 60 a mile northeast of Carrizo. There you can return to Show Low (25 miles) or turn south to Globe (65 miles).

McNary. This lumber-mill town in the pine-forested uplands of the northeastern reservation has an unusual history. Until 1923 it was

Cooley, Arizona, the site of a small mill and lumber company. In that year the operation was purchased by the Cady Lumber Co. of McNary, Louisiana, whose managers, William Cady and James McNary, were looking for a new timber supply. They loaded the company's logging and mill machinery and the families and belongings of 500 employees on two long private trains and moved the whole works to the new town built among Arizona's Ponderosa pines.

Today the company is Southwest Forest Industries. You can tour the mill, from log pond to drying kilns, with a company guide. Inquire at the company offices, south of the highway.

Sunrise ski area. The Apaches' ski resort near Greer is one of Arizona's major ski areas, now being developed as a summer resort.

The handsome 50-room lodge, on a hill overlooking Sunrise Lake to the north and the slopes of Sunrise Peak to the south, offers first-class accommodations. Lodge facilities include dining room, coffee shop, cocktail lounge with dancing, conference rooms, gift shop, and sauna.

At the ski area, a double chairlift takes skiers up Sunrise Peak for downhill runs on a variety of slopes. A pomalift and tow serve smaller slopes. Equipment rentals are available.

In summer, the chairlift provides a scenic ride to the mountain vista point. Boats and tackle are available for fishing. For information and reservations, write to Sunrise Park Hotel, P.O. Box 217, McNary, AZ 85930.

Trout hatcheries. The Williams Creek Fish Hatchery near McNary and the Alchesay National Fish Hatchery near Whiteriver both welcome visitors during daylight hours. The first is about 8 miles south of McNary. Take the road to Williams Creek; turn east below the rim. The turnoff to Alchesay is marked on State 73, 5 miles north of Whiteriver. From there it's about 3 miles by dirt road. Check directions locally; ask about road conditions after rains. Alchesay has a visitor center and picnic sites.

Lakes and streams. The western half of the White Mountain Recreation Area on the reservation, including the Mt. Baldy Wilderness Area, encompasses 26 lakes created by dams built by the Apaches' enterprise and more than 400 miles of trout streams.

The most accessible and popular big lakes are Hawley Lake, reached by paved road south from U.S. 73 about 9 miles east of McNary, and Sunrise Lake, on the road south to Sunrise Park ski resort. At Hawley you'll find a store and boat rentals. Both lakes contain primarily rain-

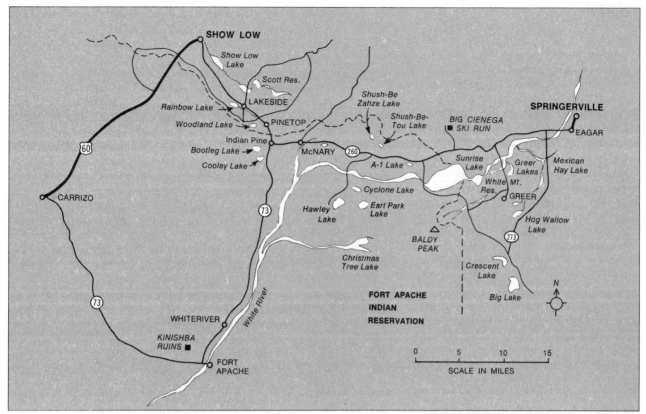

SCENIC White Mountains offer a cool forest retreat, excellent for hunting, fishing, and relaxing.

bow trout, some brook and brown trout. Near Hawley Lake, the smaller Cyclone and Earl Park lakes are reached by short walks from nearby roads.

Smaller lakes along U.S. 73 between Mc-Nary and the Sunrise turnoff—Shush Be Zahze (Little Bear), Shush Be Tou (Big Bear), Bog Creek, Horseshoe, and A-1 (right beside the highway)—are good for trout fishing and have picnic areas and campsites. Cooley and Bootleg lakes, just west of U.S. 73 by a graded road 2 miles south of the Hon-Dah motel at Indian Pine, have catfish as well as trout.

On the southern slopes of Mt. Baldy, at the eastern edge of the reservation, another cluster of lakes—Pacheta, Drift Fence, Hurricane, and Reservation—can keep a trout fancier busy for some time. You can reach the lakes by gravelled road south from Whiteriver, turning east past the Maverick Lookout. At Reservation Lake are a store and boat dock.

Christmas Tree Lake, off the McKinney Lookout Road northeast from Fort Apache, contains only the rare, native Apache trout.

The streams descending from Mt. Baldy—Hurricane and Big and Little Bonito southward, Diamond Creek to the west—also are prime trout waters. The White River, a confluence of

streams from the Mt. Baldy area, and the Black River, forming the southern boundary of the reservation, now abound in smallmouth bass planted several years ago. You can also catch trout.

On the western side of State 73 are two more fishing creeks, Cibecue and Canyon, that are less visited by tourists. To reach the little town of Cibecue on the creek, turn west off State 73, 6 miles south of Carrizo Junction. Canyon Creek, along the western edge of the reservation, is reached by jeep trails from west of Cibecue.

THE WHITE MOUNTAINS

A cool mountain vacation land of forests, lakes, and streams, this is the Arizonans' answer to the heat of July and August. It is especially appealing to hunters, fishermen, and followers of high mountain trails.

The White Mountains lie within parts of the Apache-Sitgreaves National Forest and the Fort Apache Indian Reservation. (For the White Mountains on Apache land, see pages 79-80.)

The area contains some of Arizona's finest forest land; Ponderosa pine, spruce, Douglas fir, and aspen fringe the lakes and meadows.

Show Low

The town (elevation 6,330 feet) takes its name from an early incident in which one pioneer, gambling with a ranch at stake, challenged another to "show low" and take the ranch. He showed a low card, took the ranch, and later sold it to the Mormons who opened it for settlement.

Today it's a major shopping center of the area, with many motels and restaurants, rodeo grounds (Fourth of July is the big one), and many resorts and cabins. Around it are several lakes—Fool's Hollow Lake and White Mountain Lake to the north, Show Low Lake to the south —and both Forest Service and commercial campgrounds.

North of Show Low, State 77 runs through farming and dairy country to meet U.S. 66 at Holbrook. In its course, it passes through several prim little farming communities—Shumway, Taylor, Snowflake—that have a faintly New England flavor because of their red brick homes, built in down-East style in the 1870s.

South of Show Low, State 260 cuts through the forests to the lumbering towns of Pinetop and McNary and leads into the great recreational area of the White Mountains.

Along the Rim

In the White Mountains the Mogollon Plateau rises to 11,590 feet at the top of Mt. Baldy. Most of the intervening country is at an altitude of from 6,000 to 9,000 feet.

The headwaters of three major rivers flow from the foot of Mt. Baldy: the Little Colorado flows north through the Apache-Sitgreaves National Forest; and the Black and White rivers flow across the Fort Apache Reservation. The 7,400-acre Mt. Baldy Wilderness Area surrounding the peak is not penetrated by roads, but it can be reached by trails from reservation roads and from Sheep Crossing Campground, about 5 miles south of Greer.

The rim road, a dirt road from the vicinity of Pinetop all the way west to Camp Verde on U.S. 17, offers spectacular views but often is impassable for passenger cars, particularly from Lakeside to Deer Springs.

Lake country

Thirteen lakes and 250 miles of streams cover the non-reservation lands of the White Mountains between Show Low and Springerville.

The pines beside the highway from Show Low to Pinetop harbor many resorts, lodges, rental cabins, and campgrounds. The towns of Lakeside and Pinetop have modern motels, restaurants, stores, and many commercial services. In Pinetop attractive commercial buildings harmonize with the rustic setting and the roughhewn look of earlier construction.

McNary is the home of Southwest Forest Industries' big lumber mill, offering guided tours for visitors.

East of McNary, State 260 climbs into a summit of alpine meadows. You come upon aspen-bordered A-1 Lake before the turnoff to the Apaches' Sunrise Park Lodge and ski area.

The tiny hamlet of Greer at 8,500 feet is in a secluded mountain valley 5 miles south of the highway. The winter population of about 120 swells to around 5,000 in the summer as vacationers move into lodges, cabins, and campgrounds.

At the small, man-made Greer Lakes, known for their big German brown trout, you can camp at three Forest Service campgrounds or at one campground upstream on the Little Colorado.

From the lakes a gravel road leads south to Sheep Crossing campground on the Little Colorado and trails westward into the Fort Apache Reservation and the Mt. Baldy Wilderness Area. Farther south, the road continues to Crescent Lake, Big Lake, and the creeks forming headwaters of the Black River.

You will find detailed maps of the area at local stores and lodges or the national forest headquarters at Springerville.

GRAZING COUNTRY

East of the Fort Apache boundary, the road drops to the grass-covered rolling hills and plains of Arizona's rich cattle country. The bunch-grass grazing lands, studded with dark outcroppings of lava and porous volcanic bombs, continue north past Holbrook. Farther north they yield to the harsher terrain features of the barren Hopi mesas and the red rock sculptures of the Navajo heartland.

Eagar

Named for three Mormon pioneer brothers who held out against outlaws and Apaches, the town today is a quiet ranching and farming center bearing the Mormon trademark of wide, clean streets, tall poplars, and neat houses and yards. The cattle ranch area surrounding the town is well known for purebred Herefords.

Springerville

This shopping and service center for lumber and cattle industries and for a continuing stream of tourists was not always so peaceful. During the 1870s and '80s it was one of the roughest towns in the Southwest, populated by fugitive cattle rustlers, horse thieves, and various other outlaws.

Lyman Lake

For fishing, boating, water-skiing, camping, and picnicking, a pleasant stop between Springerville and St. Johns is Lyman Lake State Park. The 1000-acre reservoir lies among rolling, grassy hills in a shallow canyon on the Little Colorado River. Fishing for bass and northern pike is good in fall, winter, and spring. Summer is the popular time for boating and skiing.

Facilities at the lake include campsites, showers, trailer pads with hookups, launching ramp, boat rentals, and a store. There's a small fee for fishing privileges.

A small herd of bison is enclosed on a hill near the highway entrance; they're frequently close by the road at the feed racks.

THE CORONADO TRAIL

Paralleling the eastern border of Arizona, U.S. 666 links the high plateau and the desert lowlands. Between Springerville and Clifton you pass through both the Blue and White mountain ranges. Although the two towns are only 117 miles apart, the highway twists and winds, stretching the distance to a 3½-hour drive, exclusive of stops and side trips.

The Coronado Trail takes its name from the Spanish explorer, Francisco de Coronado, who passed this way more than four centuries ago. In spite of its scenery, the road was lightly traveled until recent years because portions were unpaved and often closed in winter. Now an all-weather highway, it still is uncrowded.

This region ranks among the best hunting and fishing areas of the Southwest. From your car you are likely to see deer, elk, antelope, and turkeys—and perhaps even a bear—as well as countless smaller animals.

Overnight accommodations along this route are very limited. You'll find motel accommodations in Alpine, a lodge and cabins at Hannagan Meadows, and cabins at Beaverhead. There are six improved Forest Service campgrounds along U.S. 666 between Eagar and Morenci. Another

four are on the forks and tributaries of the Black River south of Big Lake, accessible from Beaverhead. On the west side of the ridge, look for the camp at Blue Crossing if you're seeking seclusion. There's another campground several miles north on the river, one near Luna Lake, and one at the 8,500-foot divide north of Alpine.

For specific information on campground locations and hunting and fishing regulations, write to the Forest Supervisor, Apache-Sitgreaves National Forest, Box 640, Springerville, AZ 85938.

Alpine

Passing Nelson Reservoir, a popular lake, you come upon the hamlet of Alpine, a pleasant crossroads village. The scenery in this area is spectacular in the fall when the white bark and shimmering yellow leaves of the aspens stand out against the deep greens of the conifers. If you have time for some off-highway exploring, consider the following side trips from Alpine.

Escudilla Mountain. The dirt road up the mountain is rough but normally navigable for passen-

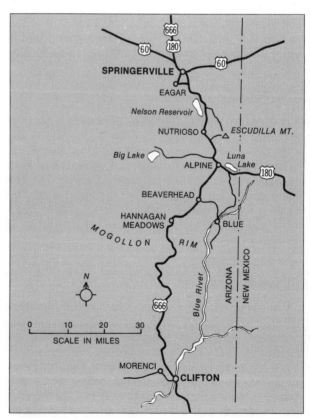

CORONADO TRAIL curves through Blue and White mountain ranges of eastern Arizona.

ger cars for about 4½ miles. Turn northeast from the highway on Terry Flat Road about four miles south of Nutrioso.

Williams Valley—Big Lake. This back road to Big Lake leaves the highway about two miles north of Alpine (see Lake country, page 82). Cattle graze on the green grass of Williams Valley, a meadow ringed with tall aspens. You can continue on any of several roads to complete a loop drive, but the best way back to the Coronado Trail is the route you just drove.

Escudilla Mountain Loop. Two miles east of Alpine you can turn left from U.S. 180 onto a graded road that will take you to Stone Creek and on around the east and north sides of 10,955-foot Escudilla Mountain. The road eventually swings up to U.S. 666 about six miles north of Nutrioso.

Blue River. An excursion into the peaceful world of the Blue River starts near Luna Lake, about 3½ miles east of Alpine. You leave U.S. 180 to curve through pastoral countryside and then drop into a wide canyon where the walls are elaborately eroded into spires and irregular cliffs.

You can continue for 14 miles beyond the Blue Post Office to road's end; or you can turn back at any point and take the Red Hill Road out to U.S. 666. The climb to Beaverhead yields splendid views back over the Blue River Valley.

The Mogollon Rim

From Alpine to Hannagan Meadows is one of Arizona's loveliest forest drives, but the really expansive views greet you at the Mogollon Rim. When you emerge on the rim, you come to a roadside rest turnout where you can enjoy the view and continue to the left or right onto the unpaved rim road. A short drive in either direction along the rim takes you into handsome groves of aspens.

Clifton-Morenci

Clifton is part of the historic Clifton-Morenci mining district. A mile north of town is the junction with a 5-mile road to Morenci and its huge open-pit copper mine. More than a billion tons of rock and ore have been moved here, and the pit is so large that it may take you a while to spot the tiny trains and trucks moving in its depths and over the distant terraces. There is a fenced overlook with a sign that explains the operation.

EXCURSIONS FROM SAFFORD

An excellent take-off spot for excursions into the quiet and beautiful country between Tucson and New Mexico is the pleasant farming town of Safford. Located on the Gila River on U.S. Highways 70 and 666, Safford is a convenient overnight stopping place for auto explorers.

Aravaipa Canyon

A quiet, cool retreat tucked away in the rugged country of southeastern Arizona, Aravaipa Canyon must have been a welcome surprise for early adventurers making their way across the uncharted Southwest.

Today the 8½-mile canyon is a carefully protected primitive area, open only to hikers, backpackers, and horseback riders.

The canyon itself is public land managed by the Bureau of Land Management (BLM) through its Safford office, but access at the west end is across private land owned by a conservation organization, Defenders of Wildlife.

The BLM controls entrance to the primitive area at both ends. Permits can be obtained by phone (602-428-4040) or by written request to the Safford District Office, BLM, 1707 Thatcher Boulevard, Safford, AZ 85546. Group size is limited to 10 and length of stay to no more than 3 days.

You can drive part-way into the canyon from the east end on a county road from Safford or Willcox without a permit. Signs mark where the primitive area begins. From here you hike.

To reach Aravaipa from Safford, drive northwest on U.S. 70. Six miles past Pima, turn left, cross the railroad tracks, and take the gravel road; you promptly leave the irrigated belt and are in the greasewood and mesquite rangeland typical of this part of Arizona. Don't let the fairly wide, well-maintained road tempt you to drive too fast. Your wheels will throw up loose rocks, and there are sudden dips.

About 25 miles from U.S. 70, you come to a junction with the road from Willcox (a route often taken to Aravaipa from State Highway 86). Turn right (northwest); now you are paralleling the sandy course of Aravaipa Creek. After passing several ranches, you come into the small community of Klondyke. The BLM maintains an information center here; the ranger will provide current road and weather conditions. The road forks 3½ miles beyond; take the left branch. (The road to the right, and another less prominent one about 2 miles farther on, lead away from the canyon to the settlement of Aravaipa.)

SUMMER CLOUDS gather over Big Lake, and sunflowers and larkspur brighten the quiet landscape in this popular summer vacation country in the White Mountains west of Alpine.

You now have about a 5-mile drive into the canyon before the road ends; drive slowly and enjoy it. This is unspoiled land—virtually the same today as it was 30 or 40 years ago.

Along the Swift Trail

Mount Graham in the Pinaleno Mountains, rising abruptly above the Gila Valley and the arid tablelands to 10,717 feet, is the highest peak in this part of Arizona. Up its eastern flank and along its ridges, a road called the Swift Trail gives access to the popular Coronado National Forest recreation area. You can take pleasant forest drives and enjoy expansive views. Here you can experience some of Arizona's best camping in five Forest Service campgrounds, miles of hiking trails, trout fishing in pine-bordered Riggs Flat Lake, and seasonal hunting for deer, bear, wild turkey, and squirrel.

To drive the Swift Trail, turn west from U.S. 666 at a point 7 miles south of Safford. This

Mount Graham approach is paved for 23 miles beyond the turnoff; it swings across a strip of desert to the foothills, then starts its winding climb out of arid, rocky terrain, studded with mesquite and prickly pear.

For fine views of distant mountains and of the desert and grasslands below, you'll come on several good vantage points. One is Heliograph Peak, the location of a fire lookout tower. A side road leads to it, and although you can no longer climb the tower, the 4½-mile detour is worth the drive for sweeping vistas of the terrain below.

Near the end of the trail is Riggs Flat Lake Recreation Area, a pleasant place for camping, picnicking, and fishing. You will also find ample opportunities for fishing in the trout streams near Shannon and Soldier Creek camps.

You can make the drive in a day; but allow more time and plan to camp if you want to hike or do much fishing.

Tucson and the southeast corner

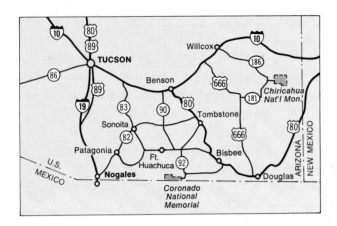

The mecca of winter sun-seekers, Tucson dominates one of the most varied and colorful parts of Arizona. Rich in Indian and Spanish history and a short drive from Old Mexico, this fast-growing town offers the cultural sophistication of a modern city while keeping the ambience of the sleepy village it once was.

During a winter or spring visit to Tucson and its environs, you can explore the mountains or the desert, afoot or on horseback. You can dip into history or archeology or shop for Indian handicrafts. You can swim, play tennis, or golf (16 courses). You can watch working cowboys on a ranch or performing cowboys in a rodeo. In the winter you can make a snowman on Mt. Lemmon—and be taking a poolside sunbath an hour later. The 2,400-foot elevation brings some chill winter spells and occasional rainstorms, but mostly, Tucson basks in year-round sun.

Tucson is unusual in its lack of satellite communities. Instead, much of the spectacular desert, foothills, and mountains surrounding the city are protected as public preserves, their extensive trails open to riders and hikers.

To the south, follow the green Santa Cruz River Valley through cotton fields, copper mines, and historic sites to Nogales, gateway to Mexico's West Coast Highway. Return to Tucson through the even greener San Rafael Valley or continue through the southeast corner on a loop filled with reminders of the days of the Old West. Here, you can stand where the

Earps shot it out with the Clantons and walk Apache trails in the rock-pillared peaks of the Chiricahuas. But you'll probably start at Tucson.

TUCSON

In Tucson you stand on flat desert surrounded by a protective ring of six mountain ranges. From the high shield of the Santa Catalinas to the close-in Tucson range, they provide a backdrop that is continually changing in hue from purple shadows at sunrise to dark silhouettes against an orange sunset.

No doubt it was the protection of these mountains as well as the water of the Santa Cruz River that attracted the prehistoric Indians who settled in this valley. Several sizable Indian communities peopled the area by the time the Spanish arrived and established their key Arizona military garrison in Tucson in 1776. Mexico gained control of the town with her independence in 1821, followed by the United States with the Gadsden Purchase and, for a brief period during the Civil War, the Confederacy. Capital of the Arizona Territory in 1867, Tucson lost that distinction to Phoenix ten years later. Today you will hear Spanish spoken as often as English along with an occasional Indian dialect, reflecting the large Mexican and Indian population.

The downtown area

A modern Community Center marks a revival of the aging heart of the city. You can find refuge here among the broad, landscaped patios separating an arena/exhibition hall, a little theater, and large music hall. A shopping plaza and hotel are part of the new look. Stop at the Chamber of Commerce down Congress Street for maps and literature.

Despite the modernization, much of the charm of the old town remains. Browsers will want to explore the specialty stores, art galleries, and craft shops tucked around the downtown area. Because the Papago reservation is close by, the choice of Papago basketry is especially good in Tucson, but you will also see weav-

"WHITE DOVE OF THE DESERT," resplendent Mission San Xavier del Bac south of Tucson,
is a handsome reminder of the time when the area was a bustling outpost of the Spanish empire.

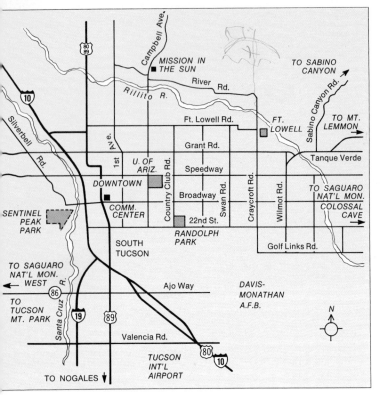

TUCSON is dramatically situated on flat desert ringed by six mountain ranges.

ing, silverwork, pottery, painting, carving, and sculpture of Navajos, Hopis, Zunis, Apaches, and others. One of the few buildings remaining from territorial days, The Old Adobe houses a restaurant and shops.

Art and crafts

Tucson's climate and dramatic surroundings have attracted artists of all kinds and stimulated development of professional and amateur talents. Works are displayed in a number of galleries. These two qualify as landmarks.

Gallery in the Sun. This unusual modern adobe, designed by artist Ted DeGrazia as a display and sales gallery, is just up the slope from the Mission in the Sun at 6300 N. Swan Road. The mission, built by the artist of desert materials, is dedicated to Our Lady of Guadalupe.

Tucson Museum of Art. This museum was created in 1975 through the efforts of Tucson's residents. It offers a permanent collection of Spanish-Colonial, Mexican, Pre-Columbian, and Southwestern paintings and sculpture. Special exhibits from their permanent collection and a crafts display are changed every four to eight weeks.

Sharing the museum's 2-acre grounds are four historic adobe houses. All date from Tucson's frontier days and will be restored by 1980. The museum's entrance lies between two of the houses: the Edward Nye Fish house, built in 1868 and now home of the Tucson Museum of Art Library, and the Hiram Sanford Stevens home dating from the 1880s.

The other adobes are the Washington-Meyer home, parts of which date to the 1880s, now used for several Tucson Museum School classes, and the Cordova House, built about 1848 (being restored as a museum of Mexican influence).

The museum is on West Alameda Street across from the city government complex. Hours are 10 a.m. to 5 p.m. Tuesday through Saturday; 1 to 5 Sunday. Admission is free.

Randolph Park

Largest and greenest oasis in Tucson is Randolph Park between Broadway and East 22nd Street west of Alvernon Way. Here are two 18-hole municipal golf courses, as well as Hi Corbett Field, spring training base for the Cleveland Indians. Exhibition games bring other major league teams to town. A zoo, tennis courts, and swimming pool offer additional recreation in the park.

The University of Arizona

Take time to visit the University campus a mile northeast of downtown. You can make a self-guided tour using a booklet available at the Arizona State Museum (just inside the main gate, Park Avenue and Third Street) or at the information desk in the Student Union. You can also pick up a calendar of campus events at the Student Union.

The campus plantings are themselves worth a visit. They comprise a subtropical horticultural demonstration—almost 60 kinds of trees, more than 100 kinds of shrubs. Most campus streets are lined with palms or olives.

Of special interest to visitors are the State Museum (anthropology and natural history); University Art Gallery (Kress and Gallagher Memorial collections); Geological Museum; nuclear reactor (at the College of Engineering); and the University Library's extensive Western Collection.

Flandrau Planetarium features more than 30 exhibits plus an hour-long planetarium show. Exhibits are open daily except Monday from 2 to 6 p.m. and 7 to 10 p.m.; admission is free. Planetarium shows are held three times each evening, Tuesday through Friday, five times on Saturday and Sunday. There is an admission charge for the shows.

The State Museum contains one of the major collections of prehistoric to contemporary Southwest Indian material. The museum is open daily but only in the afternoon on Sundays. No charge.

Arizona Pioneers' Historical Society

Just across Park Avenue from the campus, the society's library and museum features an early-day fire engine, stagecoach, and other old vehicles. Open Monday through Friday 9 to 5, Saturdays 9 to 1, Sundays 1 to 5.

Fort Lowell

This frontier army post is now a museum and public park, offering historic exhibits of Apache war days and a pleasant recreational complex including softball fields, swimming pool, playground, and ramada-shaded picnic tables.

During the Apache wars, the fort was the base for cavalry and infantry and the social center of the Tucson area, publishing two weekly newspapers and supporting a school,

church, and theater. Now the authentically restored Commanding Officer's Quarters houses a museum.

Davis-Monthan Air Force Base

At this active Tactical Air Command base—one of the most diversified Air Force sites—you can see a variety of aircraft, including an unusual collection of historic planes. Look at the display of old planes parked by the perimeter fence or arrange a tour through the Chamber of Commerce. This free tour leaves at 9 a.m. on Fridays in the winter and on alternate Fridays during the summer. The base is southeast of town on Craycroft Road.

SHORT TRIPS FROM TUCSON

Just beyond the city in any direction, you find the lively Sonoran desert of saguaro and prickly pear, creosote bush and mesquite, palo verde, countless wildflowers in spring, and the small animals that find shelter among these plants.

On three sides of Tucson, some of the most spectacular desert is protected in extensive public preserves. The Saguaro National Monument comes in two parts: the Rincon Mountain Section and the Tucson Mountain Section are east and west of town respectively. Also west is Pima County's Tucson Mountain Park. This park and the monument contain fine stands of giant saguaro cactus. The desert foothills to the north and northeast, including Sabino Canyon, are part of the Coronado National Forest.

Pinal Pioneer Parkway

For a leisurely drive to Phoenix, U.S. 80-89 takes a bit longer but offers a 30-mile stretch of especially handsome desert. Signs are limited to identification markers on desert plants; roadside rests offer shade and barbecue grills.

If you make a loop trip, driving one way on Interstate 10, you will pass Picacho Peak, the site of a Union-Confederate skirmish that was the westernmost battle of the Civil War. Picacho Peak State Park offers campsites and hiking trails.

POOLS of Sabino Creek in the Catalina Mountains offer refreshing respite from desert heat.

Mount Lemmon

If you find yourself longing for a bit of respite from a steady diet of sand, sage brush, and cactus, the mountains are not far away. The Santa Catalina, the Rincons, and the Santa Rita mountains rise so high that their upper reaches are covered with conifer forests, watered by winter snows as well as the summer storms.

The heights of the Rincons and Santa Ritas are not accessible by car, but the Catalinas are easily reached by the paved Hitchcock Highway. You drive past cactus, up through juniper and oak to the pine-covered slopes of Mount Lemmon. The drive offers camp and picnic sites, spectacular vista points, nature study areas, and, at the top, a lodge, restaurant, riding stables with rentals, and ski area. A chair lift and rope tow serve the ski area, with rental equipment available. Fine hiking trails cover the area.

Sabino Canyon

What appears to be the solid rugged wall of the Catalina Mountains is actually slashed by steep canyons on all sides. Sabino (the largest) and adjacent Bear Canyon are the only two that can be reached by automobile. (A shuttle system will go into operation in Sabino Canyon in 1979. At that time all personal vehicles will be prohibited.) In these favorite retreats of Tucson residents, you can ride or hike. You can fish for trout in the stocked Upper Sabino Creek or swim in its deep, boulder-lined pools.

You'll find four picnic areas scattered through the canyon. The visitor center is open from October to May.

Saguaro National Monument

Unique preserve of the stately, towering saguaro cacti, this site is divided into two parts, on opposite sides of Tucson. Although each section has its own individuality, both offer an intimate exposure to the fascinating desert ecology.

The Tucson Mountain Unit, northwest of the city, preserves a vigorous forest of young saguaro—the thickest stand in the U.S. Stop at the visitor center for information about wildlife, wildflowers, and cacti. You have a choice of a 9-mile scenic loop drive or 16 miles of hiking trails. Picnic areas include tables, shelters, and restrooms, but bring your own firewood. Open twenty four hours a day, this section is popular for moonlight hikes and barbecues.

In the older Rincon Mountain Unit just east of Tucson, the forest of old giants is in gradual decline because of failure to reproduce young plants. Nevertheless, a 9-mile loop drive and some good foot trails take you through majestic giant saguaros.

May or early June brings the expanse of bloom that earned the saguaro blossom the title of state flower. Plan to view these in the early morning. The pine-covered heights of Rincon Peak and Mica Mountain are accessible by trail.

Tucson Mountain Park

An 11,000-acre high desert and mountain preserve west of the city, this park includes miles of hiking and riding trails, long views of the Avra Valley, picnic sites, overnight camping areas, and trailer-camper grounds.

It's also the site of the two most popular visitor attractions in the area—Old Tucson and the Arizona-Sonora Desert Museum. The western section of the Saguaro National Monument is to the north.

Old Tucson. Both a year-round amusement park and the setting for many Western movies and television shows, Old Tucson gives you the opportunity to watch a scene in production here if you happen along at the right time.

Producers of the movie *Arizona* built the town in 1940 as a full-scale replica of Tucson circa 1860. Instead of the usual papier-mâché, painted canvas, and false-fronts of a movie set, they built it solidly of wood and adobe.

THE WILD WEST lives again in Old Tucson, setting for Western movie and television shows.

Visitors today can tour the extensive sets, ride on a replica of the Butterfield Stagecoach, tour dark mine tunnels in a clattering ore wagon, or circle the town in the open-chair cars of the Old Tucson Railroad. The old-time movie house shows silent classics and clips from films made here. Open daily until sunset. There is an admission charge.

Desert Museum. One of the best introductions you can have to the desert country, the entertaining and educational displays at the Arizona-Sonora Desert Museum—outdoors, indoors, and underground—will instruct you in much of what you will see in your later desert excursions. This living museum features the flora, fauna, and geology of Arizona or adjacent Sonora and Baja California, Mexico.

The botanical section features labeled plants in a 10-acre desert foothills complex and the Desert Museum-Sunset Magazine Demonstration Desert Garden. This unusual garden demonstrates home use of native desert plants and ideas in desert garden design.

Almost every kind of wildlife can be found in the zoo portion of the museum—from desert insects and birds to black bear, a jaguar, and mountain lions. Simulated habitats fashioned from rock-sculptured concrete are gradually replacing the fenced enclosures of the larger animals.

Popular features are the tunnel from which you can peek into the softly lighted dens of burrowing animals, the walk-through bird enclosures where an inquisitive roadrunner will cautiously approach you, and the underground limestone cave galleries of the Congdon Earth Sciences Center. You'll also find a tortoise enclosure, Prairie Dog Village, and Chulo Town (where the coatimundis live).

Allow at least two hours for your visit—half a day if you really want to see everything. A visit in the morning is cooler and the animals are more active then. The museum closes at sundown daily. An admission is charged.

Kitt Peak Observatory

About an hour's drive west of Tucson, gleaming white domes dot a crest high above the Papago Indian reservation. Here, the nation's largest federally supported observatory for research in optical astronomy occupies a site chosen over all others in the United States for its ideal star-gazing conditions.

Visitors are welcome to view several exhibits, including the world's largest solar tele-

WEST OF THE CITY, you can picnic along the drive through Saguaro National Monument.

scope observatory and a museum. These, along with a Papago crafts shop in the museum, are open daily. The drive to the peak offers sweeping vistas of the surrounding country. The town of Sells, 20 miles to the west, is the Papago tribal headquarters.

Colossal Cave

Reaching far back into the earth beneath the Rincon Mountains southeast of Tucson is Colossal Cave, colorful product of nature's patience and skill as a sculptor.

The cavern's chain of crystal-walled chambers was formed from solid limestone millions of years ago by the action of seeping water, which eventually created an underground river with an intricate network of tributaries. Today, however, the cave is bone dry, maintaining a constant temperature of 72°.

Once an Indian refuge, the cave has yielded many artifacts now on display. During the Wild West days, bandits used the cave as a hideout.

Of the miles of underground passageways in the cavern, an underground walk of about 1¼ miles is made easy by steps and walkways. A concessionaire conducts hour-long tours daily for a small fee. The surrounding area is a Pima County park and has free camping and picnic grounds. It's also a good vantage point for views of Tucson and desert sunsets.

WEATHERED REMAINS of San Jose de Tumacacori are now a national monument. In December, fiesta time at the mission brings together Mexican and Indian dancers and craftsmen.

SOUTH TO THE BORDER

The scenic hour's drive to the border town of Nogales follows the Santa Cruz River through its lush valley. On your way back to Tucson, try routes 82 and 83 for a glimpse of the beautiful ranch country of Patagonia and Sonoita.

Three colonial landmarks

Eusebio Kino, the Jesuit missionary, was the first European to enter the Santa Cruz Valley and to follow it north to the present site of Tucson. In this valley you can visit two of the missions he established and the garrison built to protect them.

San Xavier del Bac. Called "White Dove of the Desert," this twin-towered, historic mission stands on the San Xavier Indian Reservation southwest of Tucson.

Although the original chapel was destroyed by the Apaches, the present church is one of the oldest churches in the country in use.

Visitors are welcome at San Xavier any time between 6 a.m. and sunset. Franciscan brothers give 20-minute lecture-tours every hour on the half-hour (except Sunday and the noon hour). Visitors are also welcome to Christmas, New Year, and Easter Masses and to special celebrations and processions honoring St. Francis in early October and December. The annual celebration of the mission's founding is a colorful and exciting major event of the mid-April Tucson Festival.

Tubac. Established by the Spaniards as a presidio to protect the missions from Indian raids, Tubac was the staging point for the De Anza expedition to California that led to the founding of San Francisco. It languished when the garrison moved to Tucson in 1776 but became a center of mining and commerce after the Gadsden Purchase made this territory part of the United States.

Today the village is both a growing retirement community and a lively center of art and craft activity. There are studios and shops to visit, as well as a country club with golf course and excellent restaurant. A museum in the Tubac Presidio State Historic Park displays a layout of the original Spanish town and a good many artifacts from the past two centuries.

Tumacacori. The stately ruin of the mission church of San Jose de Tumacacori *(Tooma-Kah-kori)* stands beside the highway a few miles south of Tubac. Though it was once a magnificent mission, legends of buried treasure have caused seekers of riches to pillage it.

Its story began with the arrival of Father Kino in 1691 to conduct services and teach at a Pima Indian village a few miles away. After the Pima rebellion of 1751, the village was moved here. The Franciscan fathers, who succeeded the Jesuits in New Spain's missions, started building this church about 1800. It was abandoned as an active church in the mid-1800s, due to Mexican independence, repeated Apache raids, and the ultimate private sale of the mission property.

The church was made a national monument in 1908. Partial restoration was begun in 1919. Dioramas and pictorial displays depict life in its heyday, and a garden provides a retreat.

The monument is open daily; a small admission is charged per car.

Madera Canyon

In the Santa Rita Mountain section of the Coronado National Forest is this wildlife haven and cool year-round retreat. More than 200 species of birds visit the tree-shaded canyon, and each year thousands of birders come to see them among the oak, juniper, and sycamore along the stony creek. The wood from this canyon (madera means "wood" in Spanish) provided much of the lumber that built early Tucson.

A lodge that includes cabins and a restaurant often requires reservations six months in advance during the summer birding season. Two picnic areas and a campground furnish water. A hiking trail goes 8½ miles to the 9,450-foot peak of Mt. Wrightson, highest in the Santa Ritas, and a shorter, steeper trail climbs Mt. Hopkins.

Nogales

Named for the identical walnut trees growing opposite each other on either side of the border, the twin cities of Nogales face each other across the international boundary. An important center of commerce and port of entry, Mexico's Nogales retains many of the customs and crafts of old Mexico. Here you can shop in an international marketplace, feast at good restaurants amid strolling mariachis, and, if you go on certain Sundays, see the top matadors of the Spanish-speaking world in the Nogales bull ring.

Before you start serious buying, visit several stores and markets to compare prices and quality, for they vary considerably. Among the interesting wares are rugs, pottery, carved wooden furniture, tinware, glass, and leather from Mexico; perfumes and silk goods from France; cameras, cutlery, and mechanical toys from Germany; cameras and optical products from Japan; and many other imports.

Some items can be bought duty free; others are restricted. Liquor is a bargain, but you can only bring back one quart per adult per month.

Mexico's Nogales offers interesting places to sample Mexican food of a greater variety than is usual north of the border. The oldest and best known is *La Caverna*, tunneled out of the bluff facing the plaza. Seafood and game are specialties. A charming, more recent addition is colorful *El Balcon*, upstairs above the Casa Margot shopping complex.

Crossing the border. You do not need any document to cross the border but if you are going beyond the Nogales free-port zone, you must have a tourist card. You can obtain this at the border or save time by getting it in advance at the Mexican Government Tourist Office in Tucson.

Delay for customs and immigration clearance coming back averages 10 to 12 minutes, officials say, but it can run as long as 45 minutes. Inspection is strict and sometimes involves emptying the trunk of the car and opening luggage and all containers. Busiest days are weekends and Mondays.

Two lakes

For fishing, boating, and just cooling off, two lakes beckon in opposite directions from Nogales. Both drives take you quickly into the mountains and cooler temperatures.

Pena Blanca Lake. Nestled in a mountainous pocket at an elevation over 3,500 feet, mile-long Pena Blanca Lake attracts residents of Tucson and Nogales to this section of the Coro-

CROSSING THE BORDER—SOME HINTS

When you cross the border into Mexico, customs officials don't volunteer the information you will need when you return. Here are some of the basics; for unusual situations and for brochures on customs regulations, ask at the customs buildings, located near border crossings.

Declaration. You must declare anything purchased in Mexico—a written declaration if the total of fair market value or purchase prices of the items exceeds $100.

Duty. You can bring back up to $100 worth of goods except some prohibited or restricted items, without paying duty—but only once every 30 days. (Up to one quart of liquor may be included in this exemption; Arizona state law prohibits importation of more than one quart.) If you've already used your exemption within the last 30 days, you're still entitled to a $10 exemption on a subsequent trip.

Members of a family traveling together can pool their individual exemptions. Thus, a family of 4 has a $400 exemption to use as they choose. Pay duty in cash or with a personal check at the customs station on your return.

Shipping and Mailing. If you ship an item, it cannot be included in your $100 exemption. If it is small enough, mail or parcel post is easiest and least expensive. Duty is paid when it is delivered.

You can send an unsolicited gift valued under $10 duty free (as long as an addressee doesn't receive more than $10 worth in one day). Write "unsolicited gift, value under $10" on the package.

Pets. Only obviously healthy animals are allowed to enter the U.S., and these are subject to inspection and possibly vaccination and quarantine. Find out about the specific animal before you buy from the customs brochure, *So You Want to Import a Pet?*

Plants and Produce. These are subject to Department of Agriculture pest and disease controls and rigorous inspection. Some are banned or require written permits.

Trademarks. Some U.S. owners of trademarks of products manufactured abroad have registered those trademarks and restricted their import. So there are some specific items, such as perfume and cameras, that you cannot bring into the U.S. or can only bring in controlled quantities, unless the trademark is removed or obliterated. For information on these items, read the brochure, *U.S. Customs Trademark Information.*

Before you go. Register any of your own foreign-made articles at the U.S. Customs office before you cross the border and keep the certificate. You can also show a purchase receipt or other proof of ownership.

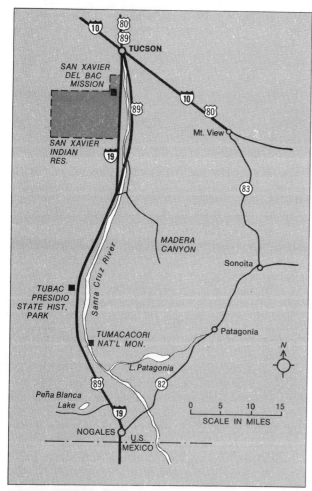

LOOP TRIP south to the border features historical landmarks and beautiful ranch country.

nado National Forest west of Nogales. Month-ly stocking of trout from November to March supplements the resident population of bass, bluegills, crappies, and big catfish. Only elec-tric trolling motors are allowed on the lake.

Beyond the lake, a gravel road winds through the Atasco Mountains to the little set-tlement of Arivaca, passing the ghost towns of Ruby, now fenced and guarded private prop-erty, and Oro Blanco. Farther on, a very rough side road turns off to Arivaca Lake, another fishing spot.

It's about 55 slow miles back to the highway through rolling grass and mesquite-covered hills studded with buttes, layered slabs of ex-posed, eroded sandstone, and volcanic pali-sades. Just after a rain, the road just beyond Pena Blanca Lake is often flooded in spots.

Patagonia Lake. Larger than Pena Blanca and high enough at 3,600 feet to be popular during

hot weather, this privately owned recreational lake lies northeast of Nogales off State 82. Op-erated by a non-profit association of area resi-dents who created it by damming Sonoita Creek, the lake has such facilities as a sandy beach, restaurant, tackle shop, boat rentals, and campsites.

Game fish stocked year round include large-mouth bass and rainbow; German brown, brook, and California golden trout; channel catfish, bluegill, and crappie. No state fishing license is required, but you must obtain a daily fishing permit. Fees are also charged for admis-sion, boat launching, camping, and trailer hook-ups. Motors are allowed on the lake, but there's a no-wake speed limit.

San Rafael Valley

The strip of border land between Nogales and the Huachuca Mountains is the elite cattle country of all the remaining Western range. The valley itself is a soft sea of grass in a setting of low hills and sharp ridges clothed with pines, junipers, oaks, and mountain mahogany.

Bird Sanctuary. Near Patagonia you pass the Patagonia-Sonoita Creek Bird Sanctuary, a 309-acre strip extending from Patagonia down-stream along Sonoita Creek for more than a mile. Because it has water the year round and a splendid bordering growth of cottonwoods, willows, oaks, ash, and sycamores—and be-cause it is located on the flyway to Mexico—both resident and migratory birds abound. More than 172 species have been recorded here. The sanctuary is bordered on one side by State 82, on the other by a gravel county road (an extension of Patagonia's Pennsylvania Avenue). You can enter the fenced area over one of three stiles on the county road side.

You are asked not to picnic within the sanc-tuary, but less than a mile down the highway toward Nogales is a shady roadside rest area.

The Museum of the Horse. Patagonia's Mu-seum of the Horse is just across the road from the old railway station. The impressive collec-tion of equine artifacts is not limited to Western horsemanship. Objects on display range from an ancient Greek chariot-horse bit to horse brasses from England, hardware collected all across America by the museum owners (the Stradling family) for three generations, and Western cowboy paraphernalia. The museum is open daily. There is a nominal admission charge; children under 12 are admitted free.

THE COCHISE TRAIL

Once the stronghold of the Chiricahua Apaches whose chief, Cochise, gave his name to the county, the southeastern corner of Arizona holds a living museum of the early West. On the 206-mile loop called the Cochise Trail, you can explore the rugged land that saw the struggles of the Indians and the pioneers.

Start the loop by turning off Interstate 10 at either Benson or Willcox. You'll find a museum and information about points of interest on the loop at the Cochise Visitors Association at Willcox (take the Fort Grant exit).

Tombstone

The glory—and notoriety—of Tombstone came suddenly and passed quickly. Tombstone achieved its prominent place in Western lore in only eight years. But in that brief period it constructed one of the West's most remarkable collections of frontier mining town buildings. These have remained remarkably well preserved through the years and are now being restored. The days of the Old West are relived in Tombstone during Helldorado Days, beginning the third Friday of October and lasting through the weekend.

The Tombstone hills were still Apache country when Ed Schieffelin first struck silver in September, 1877. "All you'll find will be your tombstone," the doubters had said. The next

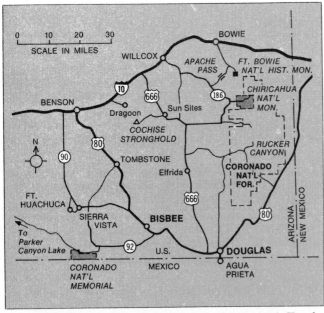

COCHISE Trail loops from Benson through Tombstone, Bisbee, Douglas, up to Willcox.

year he found more rich ore, and the rush was on.

By 1881 mining production was so great and the influx of people so large that Tombstone was a city of 10,000. It had its urban problems, chiefly disastrous fires in 1881 and 1882, and lawless strife that culminated in the showdown between Earp and Clanton factions on October 26, 1881.

Booming Tombstone became the seat of a new county named for Cochise, but it paid little attention to a growing problem that was to spell its doom—water in the mines. By the time Tombstone's resplendent new $50,000 courthouse was completed in 1882, many buckets of water were being hoisted out of the mines. The next year, pumps were installed, but production was falling, never to rise again. By 1886, Tombstone's heyday was over. The Apache threat came to an end the same year with the surrender of Geronimo.

During a stroll around town, you can stand on the site of the bloody shoot-out at the OK Corral in which the Earp brothers, with Doc Holliday, gunned down Billy Clanton and Frank and Tom McLaury (fiberglass figures show the probable locations of the protagonists); visit the Crystal Palace Saloon (its long bar is fitted out with mustache towels); the office of the Tombstone Epitaph, in publication since 1880; Schieffelin Hall, a faithful restoration of the city's biggest theater; the Bird Cage Theatre, which was Tombstone's less proper place of entertainment; the celebrated Rose Tree Inn (a Lady Banksia rose in its courtyard was planted in 1885 and spreads over 6,000 square feet); and the Nellie Cashman Hotel.

Several museums contain fascinating collections relating to Tombstone's heyday. You enter the Wells Fargo Museum through the General Store (whose specialty is old-fashioned candies). Across the street, the Schieffelin Museum has a display of rocks and minerals and a re-creation of the early mining process. The courthouse of territorial and early statehood days (in use from 1882 until 1929) is now a museum operated by the state. The Wyatt Earp Museum, operated by field historian John Gilchriese of the University of Arizona, contains an extensive collection of original records, letters, photographs, badges, and guns.

A tour of Goodenough Mine offers a fascinating glimpse of mining—all by hand—by which every bit of the high-grade ore was extracted, vein by vein. There is one tour a day at 2 p.m. The temperature is 53° all year so take a sweater (a flashlight is also useful).

Fort Huachuca

Here is a fort that has a special significance in the history of the Southwest; it is the only frontier military post in Arizona that is still active. Location of the U.S. Army Communications Command headquarters here has made it one of the more important Department of Defense installations. Its museum, in addition to displaying the collections of U.S. Army weapons and uniforms that you might expect, offers a detailed chronicling of the history of the Arizona Territory.

A large collection of old photographs, exhibits of Indian artifacts, and dioramas of various battles depicts the fort's role in the struggle between the Chiricahua Apaches and the U.S. Cavalry. One display tells about the pre-Apache Hohokam and Sobaipuri Indians. On the museum's second floor, one room is devoted to the Army's Indian scouts, the last of whom saw active service at the fort in 1947.

Near the museum building, old barracks and administrative buildings dating back to 1879 still flank the broad parade ground. Several of the original adobe quarters of the Indian scouts are still standing.

The museum is open from 9 to 4 Monday through Friday and from 1 to 4 Saturday and Sunday (closed holidays). Admission is free.

Coronado National Memorial

The first major expedition of Europeans into the American Southwest is commemorated at the point where Francisco Vasquez de Coronado entered what is now the United States in 1540. Here you can drive up Montezuma Pass for fine views or hike to the top of Coronado Peak for a sweeping overlook of the conquistador's route.

Exhibits describe the expedition and natural features of the area. There's a picnic area but no fireplaces because of the high fire hazard. You can bring a camp stove.

A gravel back road from the monument to State 82 takes you past Parker Canyon Lake, a cool retreat for fishing, camping, and picnicking (it's at 5,460 feet). This lake is stocked by the Arizona Game and Fish Department and there is a Forest Service fee. Facilities include a lodge, motel, store, and boat rentals.

Bisbee

Stacked along the ravines and gullies of the Mule Mountains, Bisbee is a proud turn-of-the-century mining town that's fast becoming a tourist favorite. Soon after copper was discovered here in 1877, Bisbee became a Phelps Dodge Company town. It remained so until 1975 when mining stopped and a productive 98-year, $2 billion era ended.

Bisbee today is rich in uncontrived nostalgia with underground, open-pit mines, and a well-preserved antique town. Explore the narrow streets of the old part of town on foot. The Mining and Historical Museum on Main Street is a good place to start. Open daily from 10 a.m. to 4 p.m. (1 to 4 on Sundays), it displays old mining equipment, dioramas, and gem and mineral collections. Pick up a free, self-guiding map of the town at the museum or at the Chamber of Commerce.

Along Brewery Gulch, O.K. Street, and their cross streets, you'll find shops and crafts galleries. There's still an early-1900s, company-town atmosphere to Main Street, west of the mining museum. The main post office and library share a native-stone building; weekdays, on the second floor, you can see a good collection of old Bisbee photographs. At number 37, the Restoration Museum displays three floors of antique clothing, furniture, and memorabilia from Bisbee; it's open daily from 10 a.m. to 3 p.m. at no charge. You'll also find craft and gift shops along Main Street.

Mine tours. Visitors are given a rare chance to confront the dark, damp, cold (47°) reality of underground hard-rock mining on an hour-long guided tour of Queen Mine inside Bucky O'Neill Hill—across U.S. 80 and half a block east from Bisbee's police station. Tours run continuously every day from 10 a.m. to 5 p.m.

Dramatic in another way is the 11-mile bus tour of enormous Lavender Pit copper mine and surrounding area. Tours are offered daily at noon and, when interest permits, at 10 a.m. and 2 p.m.; they take 1½ hours. For reservations, call (602) 432-2071 or sign up at the Queen Mine Building.

Cochise Stronghold

The name leaves no doubt: this was the great Apache chief's stronghold, a natural fortress with thousands of pinnacled lookouts from which any movement below could be seen. This is where Cochise led his people after a raid and where he needed only a token force of braves to protect the women and children.

You can now camp and picnic where Apache wickiups once circled a clearing. You'll find wa-

TWO APACHE WARRIORS

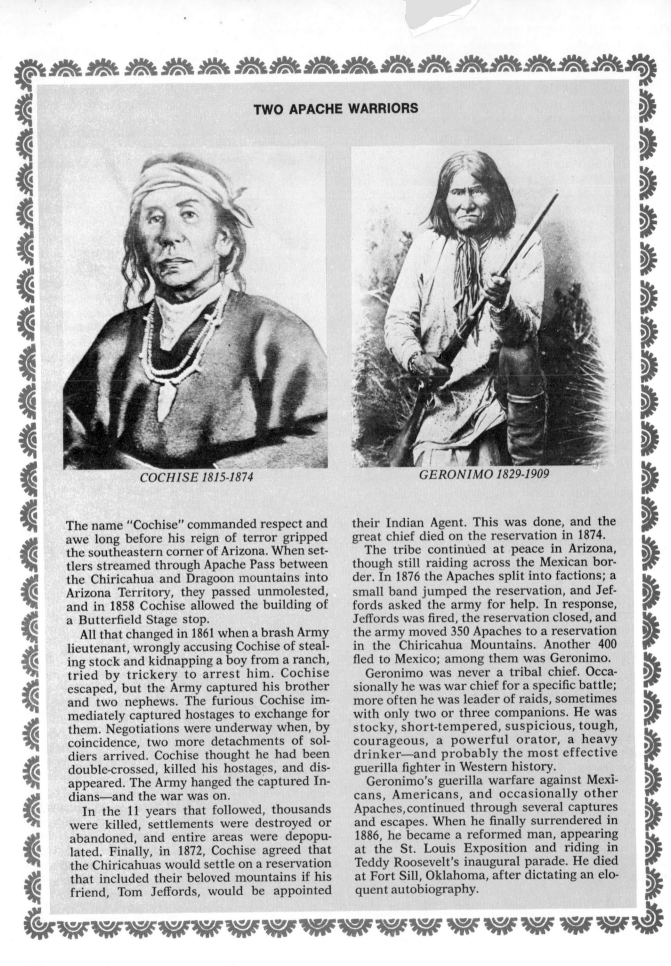

COCHISE 1815-1874

GERONIMO 1829-1909

The name "Cochise" commanded respect and awe long before his reign of terror gripped the southeastern corner of Arizona. When settlers streamed through Apache Pass between the Chiricahua and Dragoon mountains into Arizona Territory, they passed unmolested, and in 1858 Cochise allowed the building of a Butterfield Stage stop.

All that changed in 1861 when a brash Army lieutenant, wrongly accusing Cochise of stealing stock and kidnapping a boy from a ranch, tried by trickery to arrest him. Cochise escaped, but the Army captured his brother and two nephews. The furious Cochise immediately captured hostages to exchange for them. Negotiations were underway when, by coincidence, two more detachments of soldiers arrived. Cochise thought he had been double-crossed, killed his hostages, and disappeared. The Army hanged the captured Indians—and the war was on.

In the 11 years that followed, thousands were killed, settlements were destroyed or abandoned, and entire areas were depopulated. Finally, in 1872, Cochise agreed that the Chiricahuas would settle on a reservation that included their beloved mountains if his friend, Tom Jeffords, would be appointed their Indian Agent. This was done, and the great chief died on the reservation in 1874.

The tribe continued at peace in Arizona, though still raiding across the Mexican border. In 1876 the Apaches split into factions; a small band jumped the reservation, and Jeffords asked the army for help. In response, Jeffords was fired, the reservation closed, and the army moved 350 Apaches to a reservation in the Chiricahua Mountains. Another 400 fled to Mexico; among them was Geronimo.

Geronimo was never a tribal chief. Occasionally he was war chief for a specific battle; more often he was leader of raids, sometimes with only two or three companions. He was stocky, short-tempered, suspicious, tough, courageous, a powerful orator, a heavy drinker—and probably the most effective guerilla fighter in Western history.

Geronimo's guerilla warfare against Mexicans, Americans, and occasionally other Apaches, continued through several captures and escapes. When he finally surrendered in 1886, he became a reformed man, appearing at the St. Louis Exposition and riding in Teddy Roosevelt's inaugural parade. He died at Fort Sill, Oklahoma, after dictating an eloquent autobiography.

ter here, and the rocks afford a wonderful climbing playground.

The Chiricahuas

Turning east from State 181 into Bonita Canyon, you come to forested land—the ancestral home of Cochise and the Chiricahua Apaches. Cochise Stronghold, across the valley to the west, was the Chiricahua fortress; but this was their home.

The road through Chiricahua National Monument winds through scenic Bonita Canyon to Massai Point, from which there is an over-all view of the dissected lava beds that have given the area its unique forms. From Massai Point, 6 miles from monument headquarters, there are several trails through the Wonderland of Rocks. Choices range from the easy 20-minute Massai Point nature trail to the spectacular 2-hour Echo Canyon Trail. Most rewarding of all is the 6½-hour hike through the Heart of Rocks —rhyolite formations with names like Punch and Judy, Duck's Head, and Mushroom Rock. The hike is mostly downhill and ends near park headquarters. Take water and a lunch. Arrange for someone to meet you at the end of the hike; or leave your car at monument headquarters, take the shuttle bus that goes to Massai Point at 9 a.m. and 2 p.m., and hike back to your car.

Beside the Bonita Canyon road, you'll come upon a shady campsite.

A beautiful and varied scenic drive through the mountains starts with Pinery Canyon Road, the southern fork just before entering the monument.

From the Onion Saddle summit of the canyon, a side road leads south to intermittent view sites and the Forest Service campgrounds in the flowery meadows of Rustler Park. The main road drops eastward into the deep, wooded basin of Cave Creek. Seven miles below the pass is the Southwestern Research Center of the American Museum of Natural History.

The road continues east through the rose and salmon-hued rock towers and cave-pitted cliffs of Cave Creek Canyon, where there are more campgrounds and private cabins, to the little town of Portal. South from Rustler Park, a skyline trail—above 8,000 feet all the way— traverses forests of pine, fir, spruce, and aspen, skirting grassy parks and occasionally coming out on rocky points with sweeping views.

On the west slope of the Chiricahuas, you can turn off State 181 to Forest Service campgrounds far up the canyon of Turkey Creek. Still farther south is a second transmountain road giving access to Rucker Canyon and its lake, with more campsites and fair trout fishing. You can also reach Rucker Canyon from south of Apache by a turnoff from U.S. 80.

At Apache a monument marks the final surrender of Geronimo, which took place in nearby Skeleton Canyon near the Ross Sloan ranchhouse in 1886.

The Fort at Apache Pass

Apache Pass was to the early settlers a fiery baptismal into the life of Apache country. Everything bound for Tucson passed through here— the mail, the settlers' wagons, and the Butterfield Stage.

Until the fort was built, it was a gamble whether a wagon or a coach would make it through the pass. Any slow-moving vehicle was a clay pigeon for the Apaches who knew every rock and shrub. Soldiers stationed here struggled with the Apaches until peace with Cochise in 1872. Later, when the Apaches escaped the San Carlos Reservation, Fort Bowie served as the main base for the Geronimo War. Abandoned shortly after Geronimo's surrender, the few remaining ruins are today a National Historic Site.

Fort Bowie isn't easy to find, and since there are no paved roads leading up to the outpost, this is a foot trek. Check your automobile mileage at the summit sign, then start down the north slope. At 1.3 miles down the slope, look sharply on your right for a pyramidal stone monument. Set in the monument, you'll find a steel pipe through which you can sight the ruins of the fort about a mile away. The remains of its crumbling adobe and rock walls blend with surrounding earth and chaparral. From the monument, an easy 1.5-mile trail leads to the fort, where there is a small visitor center. A ranger is on duty there every day.

The Amerind Foundation Museum

You may see a remarkable collection of Indian artifacts if you plan in advance to visit this scholarly research center near Dragoon. Because the staff is busy with archeological field work and related studies, admission is by appointment only and is limited to Friday, Saturday, and Sunday. There is no charge for the tour which lasts about an hour.

Reserve at least a week ahead of time by writing to the Amerind Foundation, Dragoon, Arizona 85609, or telephone (602) 586-3003. The Dragoon Road exit from Interstate 10 will take you there.

Southwestern Arizona

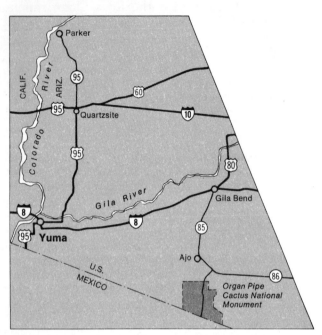

Once you leave Yuma for a mountain hike, a search for gems, or a fishing trip on the warm Colorado or Gulf of California, civilization becomes remarkably sparse. Always take necessary precautions for desert driving and hiking: carry plenty of drinking water, extra food, and good local maps.

Although accommodations in Yuma are plentiful, spring or fall desert camping is more adventuresome and offers a close-up view of desert life. Inquire locally about the condition of unpaved roads, especially if you have a camper or trailer. At some public recreation areas (Organ Pipe Cactus National Monument, for example), trailers are welcome in the developed campgrounds but prohibited on back roads and on some scenic drives. Tents with self-supporting frames offer good stability in loose sand or hard caliche and against dusty desert winds.

YUMA TERRITORY

Yuma gets more sunshine than any other city in America, declares the Weather Bureau. But in summer, on a low mesa, that's no advantage when the temperatures reach into the hundreds. In other seasons, though, the sun is a prime asset, making the Yuma area a popular vacation site.

The Yuma area offers excellent recreational opportunities: water sports on the Colorado, golf and tennis in verdant parks, desert trails for riding or hiking, history museums and art galleries, an historic prison, rodeo contest, and greyhound races. In spring you can visit the county fair and watch major league baseball teams in training and exhibition games. Outside the city, you can visit an Indian reservation or a Mexican border town, explore the Sonoran desert and mountains, take a river canoe trip, or hunt for gems.

When the Butterfield Stage crossed the southwestern corner of Arizona, weary passengers looked out at vast stretches of Sonoran Desert punctuated by isolated mountains. Passing the spontaneous spring wildflower show and hidden bighorn sheep, they eventually crossed the Colorado River into California. Travelers who parallel their route today on Interstate Highway 8 see the same arid terrain with one major change: the taming of the lower Colorado has transformed much of Yuma's desert into green fields that now yield a variety of crops.

Many natives take summer refuge from the scorching sun in Yuma's air-conditioned resorts or by the cool waters of the Colorado. Visitors, however, arrive in the autumn or spring to enjoy the pleasures of a cooler desert: a spring garden of white primrose and yellow encelia, the glimpse of a desert tortoise emerging from a brief winter hibernation, the calls of unseen wildlife breaking the still night.

With elevations at or below sea level, you can expect a mild winter and pleasant autumn and spring. Winter nights can be icy, though, and the late spring can bring high winds with the accompanying sandstorms.

MANY-BRANCHED organic pipe cactus stretches tall above a southern Arizona hillside ablaze with spring wildflowers

Yuma

Situated atop a broad mesa, Yuma dominates the southwestern corner of Arizona. The city was once a river port when the Colorado was navigable; today this lively community serves as a port of entry, county seat, and capital of an agricultural region of 200,000 irrigated acres with a 12-month growing season.

Downtown. The old Main Street has been transformed into a modern mall, partially closed to automobiles and embellished with landscaping and fountains. You'll find a modern library in an inviting park between Third and Fourth streets and Third and Fourth avenues.

For a view of the history and art of the region, visit the Yuma Historical Society Museum and adjacent galleries of the Yuma Art Center at 248 South Madison Avenue. It's open from October to June, weekend afternoons and weekdays except Mondays. Admission is free.

Yuma Territorial Prison. This notorious old penitentiary, built by convicts in 1875, stands on Prison Hill in a state historic park, overlooking the Colorado River. Today the rusty iron gates open daily to visitors who can browse in a small museum where the mess hall and chapel stood. Adults pay a small entrance fee; accompanying youngsters under 14 enter free. You can picnic in the park.

Beyond the Yuma mesa

Exploring the territory beyond the town of Yuma takes you through the green fields and citrus groves of the Yuma Valley. Much of the land that is not farmed belongs to military reservations. You can arrange for tours of portions of the Marine Corps Air Station and the Army's Yuma Proving Ground through the information officers at the bases.

On the handsome campus of Arizona Western College, about 10 miles east of Yuma on U.S. 95, the college art gallery features the works of students and guest exhibitors and a permanent collection of Indian art.

Old Mexico. Adventurous shoppers can bargain for a variety of Mexican goods in San Luis, Sonora. The shops and numerous Mexican restaurants give this border town its colorful Old Mexico ambience. Take U.S. 95 about 20 miles southwest of Yuma.

Fort Yuma Indian Reservation. The Quechan Indians or Yumas were the first to divert some of the Colorado into irrigation canals to support their crops. Today their reservation lies just north of Yuma, across the river in California.

The reservation includes the site of Fort Yuma, established by the U.S. Army in 1850. The Quechan Indian Museum now occupies the former Officers Mess, and a shop there sells Indian craft products. Open all day on weekdays, the museum charges a small admission.

Nearby are tribal headquarters, St. Thomas Mission, and a theater used by Yuma's Gondolfo Players. The Methodist Mission displays Indian dress, pottery, baskets, beaded jewelry, and dolls; some articles are for sale.

Each spring, usually the last week in March, the reservation is the site of the annual South-

IRON GATES open to Yuma Territorial Prison, built by convicts in 1875.

west Indian Pow-Wow when the Quechans are hosts to many tribes for presentation of traditional ceremonies.

Territorial trails. To familiarize visitors with attractions representative of the area, the Yuma County Chamber of Commerce sponsors a series of free, guided, drive-yourself tours of some of the most interesting sights. Several tours visit date and citrus operations; others visit the military installations. An all-day trip can take you into the desert to a ghost town, to Palm Canyon, or to a Mexican tortilla factory.

Tours start in November and continue through early April. For a schedule of the season's tours, write to Yuma County Chamber of Commerce, P.O. Box 230, Yuma, AZ 85364.

THE RIVER AND MOUNTAINS

Two large wildlife preserves cover a good part of the Colorado river and mountains north of Yuma. To thoroughly explore the unique terrain of each of these areas you have to abandon your car and go by boat or on foot.

You can drive up along the Colorado as far as Martinez Lake or a few other access points in that region, but you'll best appreciate the long stretch included in the Imperial National Wildlife Refuge if you go by boat. A couple of unpaved roads lead into the Kofa Mountains, but a view of the unique grove of native palm trees in the center of the Kofa Game Range requires a short hike. You may even spot a bighorn sheep.

Up the Colorado

Now thoroughly tamed by a succession of dams, the Colorado River bounds Arizona on the west from the Mexican border to the upper end of Iceberg Canyon above Lake Mead. The many curves and bends in the river make reference to the east and west banks rather ambiguous: the commonly used distinction is "the Arizona side and the California side."

From all over the Southwest, the river attracts aquatic sportsmen for warm-water angling (black bass, bluegills, crappies, and catfish), water-skiing (with some restrictions), scenic cruising, or camping. Boat camping along the river at spots accessible only by water is practical and popular, although no camping is permitted in the Imperial National Wildlife Refuge. Less rugged adventurers can choose

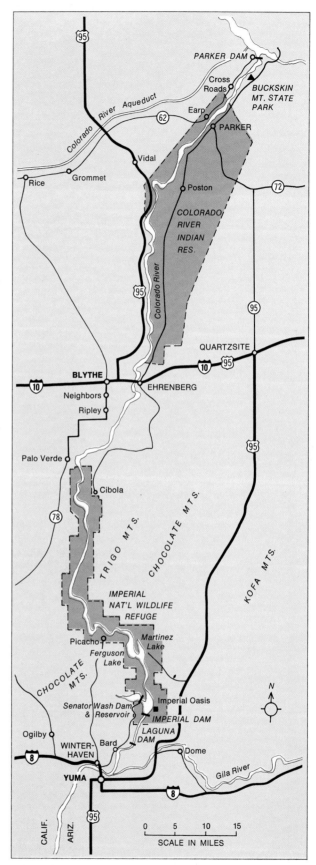

WATER buffs head for the cool Colorado; nature seekers enjoy mountains of southwestern Arizona.

HEADED FOR CALIFORNIA, water released from Imperial Dam enters All-American Canal System.

between rustic cabins, trailer parks, or car camping sites. Since mid-summer is the peak season on the river for Arizonans seeking refuge from the heat, advance reservations for accommodation and boat rentals are highly recommended. A number of commercial guides and maps covering different stretches of the river are available at marinas and fishing camps.

Imperial Dam. The Colorado River mixes work and play at the Imperial Dam north of Yuma. Here water is diverted to irrigate the land of Arizona and Southern California. But the dam also raises the water level of the Colorado 23 feet, widening the river for 30 miles upstream

and providing good facilities for boaters, fishermen, and water-skiers. Caution is advisable, though, for the water that spills into adjacent lowlands forms numerous lakes and sloughs that can be shallow, often hiding stumps and snags of drowned trees. Water-skiing is confined to the main channel, to deep water above dams, and to other waters known to be clear of subsurface hazards.

A chain of lakes. Above the dam a chain of lagoons and overflow lakes curves north to Martinez Lake, the largest in the chain. Two fishing camp-marinas offer boat rentals, cabins, camping sites, restaurants, and stores.

The river spreads into multiple shallow channels, some of them cul-de-sacs, bordered by lush stands of carrizo and tules that often conceal backwater lagoons. Great loads of silt and sand carried along by the river's currents are deposited when the river is low, blocking access to the smaller lakes.

The Senator Wash Reservoir and Ferguson Lake are popular recreation areas accessible from the California side. Most of the access roads on either side of the river are graded but unpaved and are sometimes impassable. Between Martinez Lake and Picacho, you'll find no road to the river.

Picacho to Parker. Cliffs become more prominent in the Picacho vicinity, which includes a 9-mile shoreline of state park, encompassing the ghost town of Picacho, described by Zane Grey in *Wanderer of the Wasteland*. Across from the park, on the Arizona side of the river, Hoge Rock is worth a climb for the view it affords of the rugged landscape, backwater lakes hard to see from the river, and the tule-ringed lagoon beneath you.

The Palo Verde Lagoon and Marina are often lively places. Between June and the end of November the lagoon is the scene of nighttime frog hunts. Hunters search the banks from boats equipped with lights, seeking the bullfrogs imported from Louisiana many years ago. The county park of the Palo Verde Marina provides picnic, camping, and launching facilities on Oxbow Lake.

An attractive spot for picnics and camping farther up the river is the state park campground at Buckskin Mountain between the town of Parker and Parker Dam. Facilities include semi-enclosed river bank cabanas facing volcanic cliffs mirrored in the water. A small museum displays pioneer relics, tools, and machinery of gold-mining days.

Annual river cruise. A good introduction to the stretch of the Colorado between Blythe and Martinez Lake is the annual Colorado River Cruise staged each fall by the people of Blythe. On this overnight family campout, each small flotilla of motor-boats is accompanied by an experienced pilot who allows plenty of time for exploring.

The well-organized launching begins on a Saturday morning at Blythe for the six-hour trip to the night's camp at Martinez Lake; the return cruise the next day, going against the current, takes longer. For more details about the trip and entry requirements, write to the Blythe Chamber of Commerce, Drawer 1216, Blythe, Calif. 92225.

The Kofa Mountains

Northward out of Yuma, U.S. 95 takes you past the rocky Castle Dome and Kofa Mountains, the refuge of desert bighorn sheep, the site of historic gold mines, a unique grove of native palm trees, and bonanza country for rockhounds. The Kofa Mountains take their name from the initials of King of Arizona, a gold mine that was operated here at the turn of the century.

The 83-mile drive to Quartzsite and Interstate 10, or a round-trip excursion from Yuma, with some brief off-the-road sightseeing, can give you a sampling of the country. There won't be time enough, though, for in-depth exploring or extended hiking; these require longer stays and camping. Crystal Hills and Alamo Lake are the only campgrounds in the area; elsewhere, take all necessary equipment and supplies with you—even your own campfire fuel or campstove.

Kofa Game Range. One of four refuges for the rare desert bighorn sheep, the Kofas also shelter desert mule deer, mountain lion, kit fox, ringtail cats, and coyotes. More than 150 kinds of birds have been sighted in the refuge; the most common are gambel quail and mourning doves. The desert bighorn sheep are wary and give humans a wide berth, but with patience and binoculars you may sight some of them.

Palm Canyon. Arizona's only stand of native palm trees is not as elusive as the desert bighorns, but you must be willing to do some rugged hiking to reach it. A small sign on the highway about nine miles north of Stone Cabin marks the Palm Canyon turnoff. From here a gravel road zigzags nine miles across the arroyo-cut desert to a turnaround and parking spot.

You must leave your car there near the mouth of the canyon and hike the rest of the way. Palm Canyon is actually a complex of canyons, and the principal grove of palms—40 to 50 trees—is near the head of the fourth tributary cutting into the north wall of the main gorge.

It's a rugged half-mile hike between tumbled boulders and a crack just wide enough to wriggle through. Watch your footing and be careful where you grab a handhold. Spiny cactus sprouts everywhere, and the canyon is alive with desert creatures.

You can camp at the road head; it's a choice spot for sunset watching and a good base camp for longer hikes. In April and May many of the desert plants display their blooms—yellow palo

ROCKHOUNDING

Collecting, cutting, and polishing specimens of beautiful rocks and minerals is hard to resist in Arizona, particularly in the gem-rich southwest corner. Those who have caught gem fever make Quartzsite their headquarters; shops and mineral displays there will give the novice an idea of what to look for locally. In other parts of the state you will find excellent mineral displays at the Arizona Mineral Museum in Phoenix and at the University of Arizona at Tucson.

The Harquahala and Big Horn Mountains to the east of Quartzsite and the Kofa Mountains to the south offer prime rockhounding sites. Between Gila Bend and Ajo, the Sonoran desert harbors jasper, agate, fire-agate, and all the copper minerals, but much of this is within the Luke-Williams Air Force Range, and motorists must obtain permission to leave the main road (ask at the gate 5 miles south of Gila Bend).

A rudimentary knowledge of geology is necessary in finding and identifying rocks and minerals; fortunately a number of good reference works are available on the subject. Some collectors are interested purely in adding to their knowledge of geology; others look for beautiful stones to display in jewelry.

You do not have to be an expert, however, to enjoy collecting ore samples from mines, gold bits from a stream, or a rock from the roadside that strikes your fancy. Any specimen you collect will arouse your curiosity about the geology of the desert.

Collecting mineral specimens is generally permitted in Bureau of Land Management lands and national forests (check with the ranger) but prohibited in national parks and monuments. Always ask permission on private land and military reservations.

---

verde, scarlet ocotillo, ironwood's lavender, all underscored by a carpet of wildflowers.

Crystal Hills. The only improved campsite in the Kofa Range, the 160-acre Crystal Hills Recreation Area is marked by a sign 11 miles south of Quartzsite.

You must provide your own water and fire fuel or campstove.

This area is a favorite of rockhounds looking for big quartz crystals spewed out by a volcanic fumarole. From the campsite you can also hike 2½ miles to an old Indian encampment to see rock paintings as well as scattered pieces of pottery and arrowheads.

Quartzsite. The Tyson's Well Station on the Arizona-California stage line's run to Prescott was established in 1856. The eroded adobe building, now being restored, still stands just west of the intersection of State 95 and Interstate 10. Around it, mostly to the north and west, the town of Quartzsite has grown. Its name comes from the post office established in 1896 at the Ingersoll Mill, where gold was stamp-milled from white quartz. Thus the town is named Quartzsite (the site of Quartz) and not Quartzite, the mineral.

An old stamp mill still stands on Moon Mountain Road just over a mile from the center of town. Hidden in this desert are some abandoned vertical shafts of placer mining holes. If you find such a hole, keep your distance. The apparently solid surface around it may be only a fragile crust held together by roots; the earth beneath may have collapsed into the hole.

The rockhound orientation of the town is clearly evident on the main street east of the highway crossroads. Signs identify a number of mineral and gem shops, and roadside displays include samples of minerals from domestic and foreign sources. Rockhounds from many states gather here for the annual pow-wow; since the town has only one small motel, most visitors either stay at Blythe or camp out.

Located at Quartzsite is the grave and monument of Hadji Ali, one of the 10 camel drivers imported from the Middle East in 1856 when the Army tested the ill-tempered beasts for transport in the Southwestern deserts. After the project was dropped, "Hi Jolly" remained and turned prospector until his death in 1902.

Alamo Lake. A recent recreational development in this arid region, the 4,900-acre site of Alamo Lake State Park surrounds the large reservoir on the Bill Williams River called Alamo Lake. The lakeside camping facilities include trailer hookups, good water and showers, a swimming beach, and boat launching ramp.

The fisherman will find black bass, bluegill, and catfish in the lake. Local animals include wild burros, often seen in small groups beside the road or heard heehawing in hidden canyons.

THE WESTERN SONORAN DESERT

Coming into Yuma from the west, Interstate 8 parallels the route of the wooden plank road built long ago across the shifting dunes. Although this Sand Hills area has been used as a desert setting in countless movies, such starkness is not typical of the western Sonoran desert.

East of Yuma, the dense vegetation of the Green Belt follows the Gila River and the Butterfield Stage route along Interstate 8. South of this strip, the cactus-studded hills of the Organ Pipe Cactus National Monument are typical of the Sonoran desert terrain that extends into Mexico.

The Green Belt

Thickets of mesquite and salt cedar crowd around potholes and marshes, sheltering a wide variety of wildlife in this hundred-mile-long strip paralleling the Gila River bed from Buckeye to Dateland. Administered by the Bureau of Land Management, the area is considered by biologists to be one of the finest white-winged dove nesting areas in the country.

A wide variety of other desert birds and wildlife attracts naturalists, wildlife photographers, artists, and hunters in the limited seasons. Camping is permitted more than a quarter mile from any water hole; bring your own water and

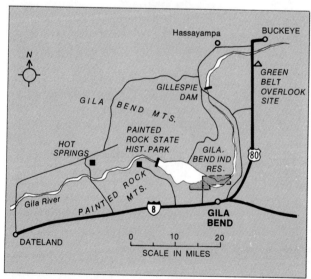

THE GREEN BELT hugs Gila River; fertile land yields crops and fruit, feeds cattle, shelters wildlife.

campstove. High boots are a precaution against rattlesnakes.

You can reach the Green Belt from a number of roads leading off U.S. 80 or Interstate 8 (see map). Many of the dirt roads are unsuitable for passenger cars. An interpretive display and overlook site is just off U.S. 80, about 6 miles south of Buckeye.

Painted Rocks. One of Arizona's richest collections of prehistoric Indian petroglyphs is preserved in Painted Rocks Historic Park north of U.S. 80 near Gila Bend.

Until the advent of the railroad and then the highway, the acre mound of rocks was a landmark on the classic route west along the Gila River. Father Kino, Father Garces, and Kit Carson all mention the site in their journals. General Kearny's army, the Mormon Battalion, and later the Butterfield Stage passed by these rocks.

Present-day Indians have no record explaining the origin of the petroglyphs, though there are several theories. The most popular explanation is that the site marked the territorial boundary and defined a permanent peace treaty between the Yuma tribe to the west and the Maricopa Indians to the east. Another theory states that this was an Indian meeting place and message center, where Indian travelers left signs on the rocks to be found by subsequent visitors.

At one side of the parking area, a sign points out the route of the Butterfield Stage, which ran through southern Arizona (see page 109).

Picnickers will find several tables with fireplaces adjacent to the parking area. There are also campsites, but no running water and no firewood.

To reach Painted Rocks, turn north from U.S. 80 about 15 miles west of Gila Bend, at the sign for Painted Rocks Dam. Follow the paved road for 10 miles to a sign that directs you left onto a ¼-mile dirt road to the petroglyph site.

Beyond the dirt road turnoff, the paved road continues for another 2 miles to dead-end at the earthfill flood-control dam on the Gila River. The low hills to the northeast of this road are choice hunting grounds for several of the copper ores and vein agate. The lake offers good boating, swimming, and fishing.

Gila Bend. This agricultural and cattle-ranching center has grown from the Gila Ranch Station established in 1858 on the Butterfield Stage route, which followed the river westward. At Gila Bend, the river makes a sharp turn toward the west.

(Continued on next page)

Just north of town, the small Gila Bend Indian Reservation is inhabited by Papago Indians. They make attractive baskets for the tourist trade.

Another way to Tucson

A leisurely trip along State 85 and 86 doesn't take you to Tucson as fast as Interstate 8 and 10, but the drive offers some fascinating winter or spring desert adventures. In the summer, plan your excursions as the desert tortoise does —in the cool morning or late afternoon.

Ajo. Commonly recognized as the Spanish word for garlic, the name Ajo also refers to cosmetic colors, and it is the latter meaning that gave the town its name. Mexican prospectors first explored the area in 1750 in response to Indians' stories of grinding up a local rock for face and body paints. The Mexicans hoped it would be silver. Disappointed at finding only copper, they continued their search for the precious metals elsewhere.

The copper boom came later with turn of the century technology, and today the New Cornelia open pit mine on the south side of town is a mile wide and more than 900 feet deep. A visitors' site on the rim offers a complete view of the great pit: giant shovels working below; ore trains puffing up the spiralling tracks; and blasting, if you're there at the right time.

Organ Pipe. Nowhere in the American Southwest will you find a more fascinating sample of the Sonoran desert environment than in Organ Pipe Cactus National Monument, home of 31 species of cactus and 225 kinds of birds, several unique to this area.

Spring is the time to see the monument's desert country at its sparkling best. In March, wildflowers perk up the scene with bright splashes of desert poppies, magenta owl's clover, blue lupines, yellow encelia, desert marigolds, and apricot mallow.

As a general rule on the desert, the larger the plant, the later it will bloom. Thus you will find the hedgehog cactus opening rose-purple cups as early as March, the ocotillo waiting until April to put on its flame-red trumpets. In most years, late April or early May is the time to find the palo verde decked out in its showiest yellow. But the giant cactus—organ pipe and saguaro—hold off until late May or early June.

Entering the monument from the north on State 85, you drive through 17 miles of park before reaching monument headquarters. The visitor center here is a good place to begin your tour and get advice on the best way to see the monument's attractions. The center is open daily, and rangers are on hand to answer questions. Throughout the winter and spring, naturalists present guided walks during the day and campfire programs in the evening.

The monument has one campground with 208 individual sites and 6 group sites. Water is available, but campers should bring their own fuel. Open campfires are not permitted.

Scenic drives. The monument has two principal roads in addition to State 85, which cuts it north to south. Both are mostly smooth-surfaced gravel with occasional dirt stretches— easy to negotiate in a passenger car.

Ajo Mountain Drive is really a nature trail for auto explorers. The 21-mile, one-way loop has numbered stakes identifying principal plant specimens and geologic features keyed to descriptions in the guide booklet you obtain at the visitor center. The best examples of organ pipe cactus are on this route.

On this two-hour drive, there are four picnic spots but no water. From the Estes Canyon picnic area you can hike about 1½ miles into Estes Canyon.

The 51-mile Puerto Blanco Drive leads you westward from the visitor center past the only known stands of the rare "old-man" cactus in the United States.

If you enjoy bird-watching, you'll want to stop at Quitobaquito Springs, where more than 180 species have been sighted.

Papago Indian Reservation. A drive through the 3-million-acre home of the Desert People reveals clusters of adobe village and glimpses into Papago culture. Most of the 8,000 Papagos who live here are involved in cattle-raising and farming, though increasing numbers work off the reservation.

In the middle of the reservation, the tribal capital of Sells houses the Papago offices, police, and a hospital, mixing modern buildings with sod-roofed adobe houses. If you need information, go to the Tribal Office or to the government's Papago Agency. An arts and crafts store, open weekdays, offers examples of the handsome basketry for which the Papagos are famous.

The annual Feast of St. Francis in Sells in October is attended by hundreds of Papagos from all over the reservation. The day begins with a mass, followed by the feast, dancing, games, and evening fireworks. Most Papago gatherings and festivals are private affairs, but the public is welcome to observe this one.

Another event open to the public is the annual Papago All-Indian Rodeo and Fair in Sells held later in the fall. Many spectators come from Tucson for this tribal event, which includes exhibits of basketry and pottery, a parade, Papago singing and dancing, and a "Miss Papago" pageant. For more information, contact the Papago Rodeo and Fair Commission, Box 837, Sells, AZ 85364.

At the village of Gu Achi, a gravel road turns west to two archeological landmarks. According to Papago legends, the Well of Sacrifice or Children's Well, just one-tenth of a mile off the paved road, is where children were once sacrificed to stop a great flood.

The Ventana Cave, 16 miles to the west, has seen human habitation for at least 10,000 years. Many of the artifacts and relics discovered there are exhibited now at the University of Arizona at Tucson. Two of the caverns have opened for visitors.

No visitor accommodations are available on the reservation, but camping is permitted for a small fee payable at the Tribal Office in Sells. Visitors should not trespass in seemingly deserted houses. Supplies are available at trading posts at Sells, Topawa, Quijotoa, San Simon, and Gu Achi.

Kitt Peak Observatory, on the eastern border of the reservation, is worth a visit (see page 91).

Topawa Mission. You reach this Franciscan mission by an eight-mile drive south of Sells through a fine stand of giant saguaro cactus. Brown-robed friars will show you through the mission church and school. Each day, school buses gather the Indian children and bring them to Topawa where they are taught in their own language and in English.

East of Topawa, you'll see the great, pointed monolith of Baboquivari Peak, 7,864 feet high. Baboquivari (babbo-*kee*-varee) is Papago for "the narrow apex." To reach a camping site in Baboquivari Canyon from which a trail climbs to the foot of the final 2,000-foot pinnacle, take a graded road east from Topawa for 9 miles and turn off on an ungraded side road. (The water in the canyon is likely to be contaminated—don't drink it.)

THE BUTTERFIELD STAGE

Interstate highways and air-conditioned motels with swimming pools have brought Arizona travel a long way from rugged stagecoach days.

Chartered in 1858 with a $600,000 annual government subsidy, the Butterfield Overland Mail swung a 2,800-mile loop from Tipton, near St. Louis, south through Little Rock, El Paso, Tucson, Ft. Yuma, and San Diego to San Francisco. The schedule was twice a week, 25 days end-to-end, for a fare of $150 (or 10¢ a mile for shorter segments).

The route crossed Arizona from the east near San Simon through the risky Apache Pass to Dragoon Springs, northwest to Tucson and up the Santa Cruz Valley to the Gila River, then along the river and west to Ft. Yuma.

On the eastern part of the line, the coaches were the classic, cumbersome Concords, but farther west they often were replaced by wood-framed, canvas wagons—lighter, faster, and less likely to upset.

It was a grueling trip. The nine passengers crowded on three hard benches felt every rattling rock and rut as the coach lurched and swayed. Motion sickness was common, and swirling clouds of dust choked the occupants. Extra passengers on top had it worse.

A weary traveler could stay over at one of the regular stops but might get stuck there, for stage after stage might go through with no space.

Between-town stops in the Southwest typically were primitive adobe or native stone shelters, dirt-floored and furnished with packing crates and crude tables. A crew of 8 to 10 armed men guarded these tiny fortresses against Indians. The menu usually was salt pork or dried beef, beans (probably mesquite), corn bread, and corrosive coffee. This occasionally was varied when someone bagged a deer or antelope or when, through an accident, the company lost a mule.

Mishaps were frequent. Stages overturned or broke down, rains and floods blocked the trail, or raiding Indians struck. In spite of the rigors, though, the Butterfield line was the main transcontinental public transportation for three years until the Civil War interrupted its eastern service and caused its closing in 1861.

Today it is celebrated fondly as a romantic element of the frontier saga—by people who never had to ride it.

Index

PHOTOGRAPHERS

Arizona Historical Society: 2. **Craig Aurness:** 63, 66 bottom. **Richard Weymouth Brooks:** 57 bottom left. **Robert Casper:** 31. **Glenn Christiansen:** 41, 47, 48; back cover, left. **Bob Clemenz:** 39. **Ron Cohen:** 18 top, 18 bottom left, 18 center right. **Ed Cooper:** 24. **Terry Eiler:** 15. **Carroll Ann Hodges:** 40. **Philip Hyde:** 10, 18 bottom right. **Dorothy Krell:** 87, 92 top; back cover, right. **Nyle Leatham:** 55 bottom. **Paul V. Long:** 66 top. **Jack McDowell:** 73, 104. **Dana Morgenson:** 34. **David Muench:** 23, 32, 50, 76, 85, 89, 101. **Josef Muench:** 9, 16-17, 56 left, 56 right. **Don Normark:** 92 bottom. **Charles O'Rear:** 55 top, 102. **Norman A. Plate:** 91. **Robert Potts:** 56 center bottom, 57 top right, 57 bottom right. **Rancho de los Caballeros:** 64. **Betty Randall:** 56 center top, 57 top left, 57 top center left, 57 top center right. **Richard Rowan:** 33, 90. **James Tallon:** 26, 58. **Darwin Van Campen:** 74. **Robert Wenkam:** 42.